Fleecie Pets

Fleecie Pets

Easy-to-make cuddly animal friends

Fiona Goble

Watson-Guptill Publications / New York

First published in the United States in 2007 by
Watson-Guptill Publications,
Nielsen Business Media, a division of The Nielsen Company
770 Broadway, New York, NY 10003
www.watsonguptill.com

ISBN-10: 0-8230-9993-8
ISBN-13: 978-0-8230-9993-1

Library of Congress Control Number: 2006936443

Manufactured in Singapore

First printing, 2007

1 2 3 4 5 / 11 10 09 08 07

Contents

Introduction

This collection of soft and adorable fleecie creatures, each about 10 in. (25 cm) tall, will appeal to soft-toy and animal lovers of all ages.

They are made from soft polyester fleece, which is readily available and reasonably priced, and are dressed in outfits made from the same fabric or from remnants of printed cottons and sport weight yarns.

Unlike many soft toys, they are unbelievably quick and simple to make, and you only need basic sewing and knitting skills to achieve great results. There are no minuscule gussets or tiny limbs to sew on because each Fleecie Pet is made from just two main pieces. The feet and ears are part of the main body piece and are simply folded and stitched in place once the animal has been stuffed.

As well as full-sized templates and instructions for making the 12 featured Fleecie Pets and their outfits, this book also includes details for making a wide range of accessories. There are also plenty of ideas for taking the concept a step further in The Fleecie Pet Workshop, including how to customize your animal and even design your own creature.

I hope you enjoy browsing through this book and deciding which animal you want to make first. Above all, I hope you will have fun and be proud of your results!

Fiona Goble

Tools and Materials

TOOLS

Before you start making your first Fleecie Pet you will need some basic sewing and knitting equipment. Some things you will probably have already, and other items you may need to buy.

Access to a photocopier, thin cardboard, and adhesive tape

The easiest and most accurate way to transfer your Fleecie Pet templates is to photocopy the templates onto thick paper or thin cardboard. Alternatively, you can use a sheet of tracing paper. The body and head templates are separate, so you will also need some adhesive tape to fasten them together before cutting them out (see page 11).

Sewing machine and sewing machine needles (1)

You can easily sew your Fleecie Pets and clothes by hand, but a sewing machine will make it much quicker. All you need is a machine that does a basic running stitch, although one that also does a zigzag stitch will be useful for giving a professional finish to some of the clothes. Your machine should be fitted with a needle suitable for medium-weight fabrics. A size 11 or 12 (European size 70 or 80) needle is ideal. It's a good idea to have a few available, as machine needles can bend or become blunt quite easily and you will need to replace them fairly often.

Needles for hand sewing (2)

You will need three types of hand-sewing needles to make your Fleecie Pets. These are a standard sewing needle, an embroidery needle, and a tapestry needle.

You will need a standard sharp-pointed sewing needle for hand sewing your Fleecie Pets and clothes. Even if you are sewing by machine, you will need a hand-sewing needle like this for sewing the animals' feet and ears, fixing the patches featured on some of the animals and closing the gap used for stuffing. A medium-sized needle is fine—choose one that is not so thin that it bends easily but not so thick that it is hard to push through your fabric.

To embroider your Fleecie Pet's features you will need an embroidery or crewel needle. This is a medium-length sharp-pointed needle that has an eye large enough for you to thread with embroidery thread.

For making the Fleecie Pets' pullover sweaters and knitted accessories, you will also need a tapestry needle. These are thick, blunt needles with an eye large enough to be threaded with two-ply yarn.

Iron

When making the Fleecie Pets' clothes you will need an iron to press open seams, fix fusible webbing and appliqués, and give a professional finish to some of the finished items.

Water-soluble pen or quilter's pencil (3)

You will need a water-soluble pen or quilter's pencil to draw around the templates and to mark the toys' features before you embroider them. They work like ordinary pens or pencils, but the marks are easily removed by spraying or dabbing with water. The pens usually come in bright blue and are the best choice for marking lighter-colored fabrics. For darker fabrics, choose one of the pencils that come in a range of light colors, including white, yellow, and blue. Water-soluble pens and quilter's pencils are widely available in craft and notions stores, and through mail order companies and Internet sites that supply accessories for quilting.

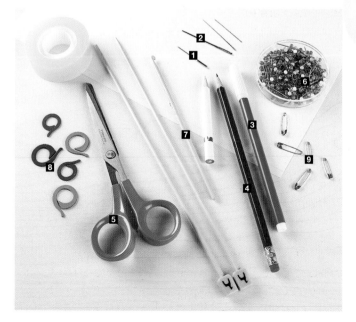

Ordinary lead pencil (4)

You will need a pencil for tracing the appliqué shapes featured on some of the clothes onto the backing paper of your fusible webbing (see page 10). A pencil is also useful for pushing the polyester fiber into the Fleecie Pets' limbs when you are stuffing them.

Scissors (5)

Ordinary scissors are fine for cutting out your pattern paper, but you will need a pair of good-quality sewing scissors for cutting fabric. Make sure that you keep them strictly for cutting fabric, as using them on paper or cardboard will quickly blunt them.

Dressmakers' pins (6)

You will need a small number of dressmakers' pins to pin your work together before basting or sewing. It is a good idea to use pins with colored glass ends. These are much easier to see, and therefore less likely to get left in your work by mistake.

Knitting needles and crochet hook (7)

To knit the Fleecie Pets' pullover sweaters and some of the accessories you will need a pair of size 5 (3.75 mm) knitting needles. For Spangles the Cat's handbag and the knitted cape in the Accessories section you will also need a size 6 (4 mm) crochet hook.

Row markers (8)

A set of row markers is useful to mark certain places in your work when knitting the Fleecie Pet pullovers. Alternatively, you can use some small safety pins.

Safety pin (9)

You will need a small safety pin to thread the elastic cord through the waistband casings of the Fleecie Pets' pants, shorts, and skirts.

MATERIALS

All the materials you need to make the Fleecie Pets are readily available in fabric stores and notions stores or from mail order and Internet companies. The main fabric used for the Pets themselves is polyester fleece—sometimes called polar fleece. This is the fabric used to make items such as fleece pullover sweaters and hats. You will also need polyester fiber to stuff your Fleecie Pets and

embroidery threads for their features. Depending on which animal you are making, you will also need different fabric for their clothes, two-ply yarn for pullover sweaters and accessories, and a selection of trims. The exact materials needed to make each Fleecie Pet are given on the individual project pages. See the following page for a photo of the materials described below.

Fleece fabric (1, overleaf)

The Pets and some of the clothes and accessories are made from polyester fleece fabric. Fleece fabric comes in different thicknesses and finishes. It varies from smooth, thin fabrics used for lightweight tops to thick, shaggy fabrics used for winter jackets. Light to medium fleece is the ideal fabric for making Fleecie Pets, as very thin fabrics tend to be too stretchy and thick fabrics are too bulky and difficult to work with.

Fleece fabric in a good range of neutral colors is available in many fabric stores. But don't worry—if there isn't a fabric store in your area, fleece is also available by mail order or over the Internet.

If you want an even greater choice of colors and textures, you could look at fleece clothing in discount clothing stores and in secondhand stores. You could even transform your own old clothes into Fleecie Pets!

Polyester fiber (2, overleaf)

100% polyester fiber is manufactured specially for stuffing soft toys, cushions, and other handmade items. It is widely available in craft and notions stores. Always check that the filling you are buying is marked safe and washable and that it conforms to safety standards.

Plain and printed cottons (3, overleaf)

For many of the Fleecie Pets' clothes you will need small amounts of plain or printed fabrics in 100% cotton or cotton blends (mixes of polyester and cotton). You don't need to use exactly the same fabric shown in the project, but for printed fabrics, small designs and prints work best. You can find these in fabric stores, craft stores, quilting supply stores, and mail order and Internet companies.

Knitting yarns (4, overleaf)

The Fleecie Pets' pullover sweaters and knitted accessories are made from sport weight yarn. It is very important that you use good-quality sport weight yarn that is at least 40% wool. Some cheaper acrylic yarns can be flat and heavy and will give disappointing results.

Embroidery thread (5)

The Fleecie Pets' eyes, noses, mouths, and paws are embroidered with 100% cotton stranded embroidery thread. This is made up of six strands that can be easily separated. For the projects in this book you will work with three strands. The color used depends on the Fleecie Pet you are making, and these details are included on the individual project pages. Black thread works well in many cases, but for lighter fleece, dark gray or dark brown is best.

Sewing thread (6)

Whether you are sewing with a machine or by hand, you will need standard sewing threads in colors to match all your fabrics. Threads made from 100% polyester, often called "all purpose," are widely available and come in a wide range of colors.

Specialty fabrics (7)

For some of the Fleecie Pets you will need fabrics such as cotton knits (the sort of fabric used for T-shirts), polyester netting (used to make tutus), acrylic sheepskin lining, and ripstop nylon (used to make lightweight rain gear). The precise requirements are given on the individual project pages. If you can't find the fabric you need in your local fabric store, you can buy it by mail order or over the

Internet. Alternatively, you can recycle items from second hand clothes stores or even your own wardrobe.

Elastic cord (8)

You will need narrow elastic cord to thread through the narrow waistband casings of the Fleecie Pets' pants, skirts, and shorts. This is widely available and comes in black or white. As the elastic usually will not show, it doesn't really matter which color you use.

Fusible webbing (9)

For some of the clothing you will need a small amount of fusible webbing to fasten the appliqués. Fusible webbing is a thin web of dry glue that is fixed on a paper backing. It is ironed onto the reverse side of the fabric. The shape for the appliqué is drawn on the paper backing with a lead pencil and then cut out. The backing can then be peeled off and the appliqué pressed in place with an iron. There are several brands of fusible webbing available, and it is widely available in craft and notions stores.

Buttons and trimmings (10)

For some of the clothes and accessories you will need small buttons, snap fasteners, and small amounts of ribbon. If you don't have these in your workbox, you can buy them in your local craft or notions store. Secondhand stores are also a good source of buttons and sometimes other items at very reasonable prices.

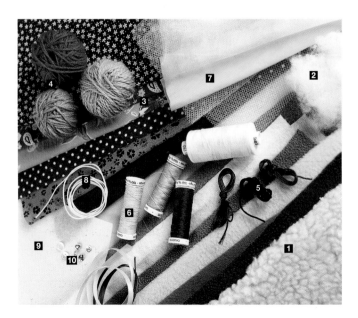

Safety It is very important that you do not give any Fleecie Pets with added extras, such as buttons, to children under three years old, as these can be a choking hazard. All the Fleecie Pets and clothes can be adapted to suit younger children. For example, the buttons and snap fasteners on Rumble the Bear's dungarees can be omitted and the straps sewn to the bib of the dungarees instead. The button on Spangles the Cat's pullover sweater can simply be omitted, as well as any pipecleaners that are used in the Pets.

Techniques

PREPARING YOUR TEMPLATES

All the Fleecie Pets in this book are made with the same body template—it is only the head templates that differ. The easiest way to prepare your template is to use a photocopier. Simply photocopy the body piece and the head piece of your choice (see pages 84–94) onto thick paper or thin cardboard, cut them out, and join them together at the neck edges with a small piece of adhesive tape. If you don't have access to a photocopier, you can trace the body on a piece of tracing paper and trace the head of your choice in the correct position. You can then cut out a single pattern piece.

TRANSFERRING YOUR TEMPLATE TO YOUR FABRIC

The easiest way to transfer your pattern is to hold the template firmly in position on the reverse side of your fabric and draw around it using a water-soluble pen or quilter's pencil. You can use the same pen or pencil to mark the position of the body dart. Simply poke the pen point or pencil tip through the cardboard template to mark the small circles—or make a hole in the template first using a large needle.

> **Tip** Whether you are shaping ears or feet or embroidering the facial features or claws, secure your thread at the beginning and end of your work by making two or three tiny stitches into the side seam and pulling them tightly. These stitches will be virtually invisible. If you are using a dark embroidery thread on a light fabric, you may find it easier to secure your thread in a place where it will be hidden by the Fleecie Pet's clothes. For example, when embroidering the facial features, secure the thread in the seam at the base of the neck.

BASIC SEWING SKILLS

If you are sewing your Fleecie Pet by machine, you will need to use a medium-length running stitch to sew your Fleecie Pet together and stitch the clothes. The fleece clothes also have a small zigzag stitches around some of the raw edges, although this is optional.

If you are sewing by hand, use a standard sharp-pointed sewing needle and a small running stitch. Work a small back stitch every few stitches for extra strength.

The Fleecie Pets' ears, feet, and any patches are always worked by hand using a standard sharp-pointed sewing needle. You also need to close the gap used for stuffing.

Embroidering eyes, nose, and mouth

The Fleecie Pets' features are embroidered after the animal has been stuffed and shaped. The features are embroidered with three strands of embroidery thread, using the same color throughout. This will be either black, dark gray, or dark brown, depending on the animal you are making.

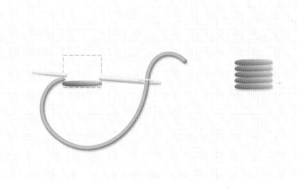

Satin stitch

Most of the Fleecie Pets' noses are worked in a basic straight satin stitch. This is a series of running stitches worked closely together so that the area is completely covered. Remember to take care to keep the stitches smooth and the length and tautness even (see above).

Some of the Fleecie Pets' nostrils are marked by a stitch called a French knot. To make a French knot, bring your needle out in the position where you want the

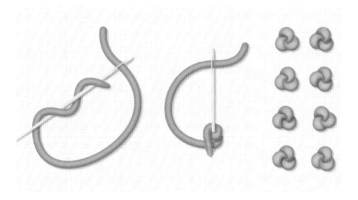

French knot

Backstitch

knot. Wind your thread twice around the needle as shown in the illustration above, keeping the needle as close as you can to the fabric. Insert the point of the needle back through the fabric, right by your starting point. Now gently push the threads down the needle and pull your thread through (see above).

The Fleecie Pets' mouths are worked in simple back stitch—each back stitch should be about 1/8 in. (3 or 4 mm) long (see above right).

Stuffing your Fleecie Pet and closing the gap

Always use a small amount of polyester fiber at a time when you are stuffing your Fleecie Pet. Also, try not to push each portion in too hard or your Fleecie Pet will look lumpy. You will need to stuff your Fleecie Pet's head firmly. This will allow you to ease the face into shape as you go. The body and limbs should be stuffed less firmly so that your Fleecie Pet has a nice, squashy feel. You will probably find it easiest to stuff the head first, then the legs and arms, and finally the torso. You can push the stuffing into the Fleecie Pet using the blunt end of a pencil or something similar—but make sure you don't use anything too sharp or push too hard or you may break the stitching.

When you are satisfied with the look of your Fleecie Pet, sew up the gap using slip stitches. Following the line of the seam, pick up a tiny amount of fabric on one side with your needle. Then pick up a tiny amount on the opposite side, about 1/8 in. (3 mm) farther along. Work a few stitches like this at a time before pulling your thread taut. Continue in this way until the gap is fully closed (see page 13, top left).

BASIC KNITTING SKILLS

For knitting the Fleecie Pet pullover sweaters and accessories, you will need to know some simple knitting techniques, such as how to cast on and bind off, and work knit and purl stitches. You will also need to know how to increase and decrease the number of stitches on your needle (see Knitting abbreviations, page 13).

You will also need to know how to piece the knitted garments together and conceal any loose ends neatly. Because the garments are small, the best method to use is called weaving, or mattress stitch. Using a tapestry needle and the yarn you have used for knitting the garment, join the side seams by inserting the needle on the reverse side under the horizontal loop by the edge stitch of one piece and then under the corresponding horizontal loop in the second piece (see page 13, top right). For shoulder seams, the pieces are joined in a similar way, inserting the needle under the knitted stitch of one piece and then under the corresponding knitted stitch of the second piece.

If you want to find out more information about knitting techniques, there are many books available on the subject and several Internet sites where you can find the information for free.

A word on gauge

The gauge of a piece of knitting is a way of expressing how many stitches and rows there are in a particular-sized square of the work. Getting the gauge right means that the finished item will be the right size. All the garments and accessories in this book have a fairly taut look to them because this looks better on items that are so small.

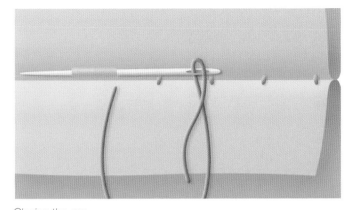

Closing the gap

Joining knitted pieces

To make sure your gauge is correct, you should knit a sample square or swatch. Using size 5 (3.75 mm) needles and sport weight yarn, cast on 10 stitches. Work 12 rows in stockinette stitch, then bind off. Your finished swatch should measure 1¹/₂ x 1¹/₂ in (4 x 4 cm). If your gauge is noticeably tighter or looser, try using needles that are one size larger or smaller.

Knitting abbreviations

The following knitting abbreviations are used in the knitting instructions for the Fleecie Pets' clothes and accessories.

alt = alternative—as in every alt row

beg = beginning

inc = increase—as in inc 1 stitch (Sometimes you will need to increase the number of stitches on your needle by knitting or purling into a stitch as usual, but keeping the stitch on your needle instead of slipping it off, then knitting or purling again into the back of the stitch.)

k = knit (This is the basic knitting stitch. The knitted fabric created by working rows of knit stitches is called garter stitch. A few rows of garter stitch are worked at the bottom edges of the pullover sweaters and sleeves to give the garments a firmer edging. Garter stitch is also used for some of the accessories.)

M1 = make one stitch (Sometimes you will need to make a stitch by picking up the strand of yarn lying between the

stitch just worked and the next stitch and working into the back of it.)

p = purl

ssk = slip 1, slip 1, K1 (This is another way of decreasing and results in a stitch that slants to the left and is a mirror image of knitting 2 stitches together. Start by slipping 1 stitch and the next stitch separately onto your needle as if you were beginning to knit them. Then, using the left-hand needle, knit through the front loops of the 2 stitches together.)

st st = stockinette stitch (This is the name given to knitted fabric that has been created by knitting one row then purling one row. It is the main stitch used for the Fleecie Pet pullover sweaters and some of the accessories. The right side of the fabric is the knit side.)

st(s) = stitch (stitches)

tog = together—as in k2tog or p2tog (Sometimes you will need to knit or purl 2 stitches together in order to decrease the width of your work. Knitting 2 stitches together results in a stitch that slants to the right.)

BASIC CROCHET SKILLS

The only crochet you will need to know is how to make a chain. This stitch is used only for the handle and button loop of Spangles the Cat's handbag (see page 55) and for the ties at the neck of the cape in the Fleecie Pet Accessories chapter (see page 76).

To start a chain from the end of a piece of knitting, insert your hook through the last knitting stitch. Draw the tail of yarn around the hook and use the hook to pull it through the loop. Pull fairly firmly. Repeat this simple process for the required number of chains or until your chain reaches the required length, taking care to keep your chains an equal size. When you have finished, simply pull the strand completely through the final loop. To make a chain beginning with a loose strand of yarn, start by making a slipstitch on your crochet hook in the same way as you would for casting on knitting (see below).

A NOTE ON MEASUREMENTS

All the measurements in the projects are given in inches and fractions of an inch with metric units (millimeters or centimeters) given in brackets afterwards. It is difficult to convert small measurements exactly, so figures have been rounded up or down. Because the conversions are not exact, it is important that you follow only one system of measurement rather than mix the two.

Making a crochet chain

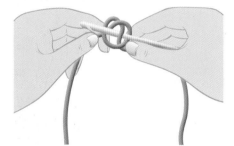

1   Make a loop with your yarn and push your crochet hook through the loop.

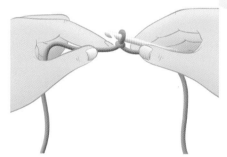

2   Pull gently on the yarn ends to tighten. This will form your first loop.

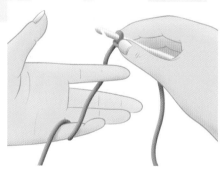

3   To hold your work firmly, loop the yarn around your little finger, take it across your palm, and put it behind your index finger.

4   Holding the base of your first loop with your thumb and middle finger to keep it steady, pass your hook under the yarn.

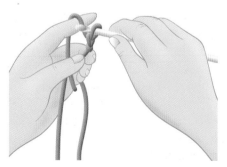

5   Use the hook to pull the yarn through the loop already formed and let your first loop drop.

6   Continue making stitches in this way to form a chain.

Starting a Fleecie Pet

Nearly every Fleecie Pet is started in the same way before you go on to give each one its unique features and clothes. Follow these 5 simple steps for each Pet and then turn to the individual project pages for the final instructions.

Check each Pet's list of materials to see what kind of fleece and templates are required before you begin.

1 Photocopy or trace the body template on page 85 and the appropriate head template (see pages 84–94) and cut them out. Tape the head to the body (see page 11). Place one of the pieces of fleece facedown on a hard, flat surface. Pin the template onto the fleece or hold it firmly in place and trace around it using the water-soluble pen or quilter's pencil. Make sure that any obvious pile runs down the length of the Pet shape, from the ears to the tips of the toes. Mark the position for the body dart with the water-soluble pen. Now cut out the shape. Remember, you only need to cut out one shape at this stage. This is called the Pet shape.

2 Fold the shape in half lengthwise, so that the fleecy side (the right side) of the fabric is on the inside. Sew the body dart—from the tip of the nose into the neck, then from the neck outward to the stomach—using a small running stitch or medium-length machine stitch. The body dart is a seam that creates a shape; for the Fleecie Pets it shapes the neck and chest of the toy.

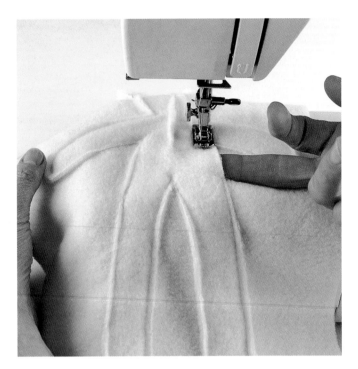

3 Lay the Pet shape down on the second rectangle of fleece so that the fleecy sides (the right sides) of both pieces are facing each other. Make sure that any obvious pile runs down the length of the second piece of fabric in the same direction as the fleece on the Pet shape. Secure the two pieces of fabric together with pins and, if preferred, baste the pieces together with large running stitches. Then machine stitch or sew around the Pet shape, 1/4 in. (4 mm) from the outside edge, leaving an opening at one side for stuffing, as shown on the template.

If you are sewing by machine, you will get the best results if you sew from the left side of the waist to the crotch first, then from the right side of the waist to the crotch. Then rejoin your thread at the left side of the waist and complete. This will avoid any tendency for the fabric to slip and will ensure that you get professional-looking results.

4 Trim away excess fabric on the second piece of fleece to match the Pet shape, taking care not to cut through the stitching. Make a snip in the seam allowance at the Pet's crotch, taking care not to cut into the stitching. This will prevent any puckering around the crotch on the finished toy.

5 Turn the Pet right side out through the gap in its side. Now stuff the Pet with the polyester fiber. Stuff the head firmly, easing the face into shape as you go and remembering not to stuff the ears. Stuff the body and limbs less firmly so the finished Fleecie Pet will have a nice, squashy feel. Then sew up the gap using slip stitches.

The following Fleecie Pets will need an additional step to add patches or to shape the face during these initial steps.

Patches the Dog

After step 2: Position the leg patch on the pattern piece, about halfway down one leg, making sure that the straight edge of the patch lines up with the outer raw edge of the leg. Topstitch the patch onto the leg using small stitches that should be virtually invisible on the finished patch. (The eye patch is sewn on after the dog has been stuffed.) See page 84 for patch template.

Squealy the Piglet

After step 2: Cut out a small oval snout and place, fleece side up, on the face. It should be in the center of the face with the top edge of the snout 1 in. (2.5 cm) below the top raw edge of the head. Baste the snout in position and sew around it, very close to the outside edge, using small backstitches or short machine stitches.

Joe the Monkey

After step 2: Place the face template (see page 90) on the reverse of the beige fleece, making sure that any pile runs down the length of the face, and pin it to hold it down. Draw around it using the water-soluble pen and cut it out. Position the face on the head so that the lower edge of the face is in line with the neck and baste in place with large running stitches. Machine stitch around the entire face, close to the edge, or topstitch using matching colored thread and small stitches that should be virtually invisible.

Spangles the Cat

After step 1: Cut out the patches from the white fleece and position the patches as shown on the template (see page 88), making sure that the outer edge of the patches line up with the outer raw edge of the face. Topstitch the patches onto the face with white thread, using small stitches that should be virtually invisible.

Patches the Dog

With his laid-back attitude and smart nautical stripes, Patches likes nothing better than messing around in boats—but always wears his flotation armbands just in case. In a soft shade of milky coffee with splashes of dark cocoa, Patches will make a loyal and faithful companion for any dog lover and won't ever need to be taken for a walk.

MATERIALS

For the dog

- 2 pieces of pale brown fleece, each measuring 9 x 13 in. (22 x 34 cm) (if the fleece has an obvious pile, this should run down the longer length of the fabric)
- Small scrap of dark brown fleece for the patches
- Matching colored threads for both fleece colors
- $^1/_2$–$^3/_4$ oz. (15–20 g) polyester fiber
- Black embroidery thread

For the swimsuit and flotation armbands

- Piece of striped navy/white cotton jersey, approximately 6 x 9 in. (15 x 22 cm) (the stripes should run across the longer length of the fabric)
- 2 rectangles of orange polyester or nylon fabric (such as that used for lightweight raincoats), each measuring 3 x 4$^1/_2$ in. (7 x 11 cm)
- Small amount of polyester fiber
- Matching colored threads for both fabrics

TOOLS

- Access to a photocopier or a sheet of tracing paper and pencil
- Scissors
- Adhesive tape
- Dressmakers' pins
- Water-soluble pen or quilter's pencil
- Sewing machine (optional)
- Sewing needle
- Embroidery needle

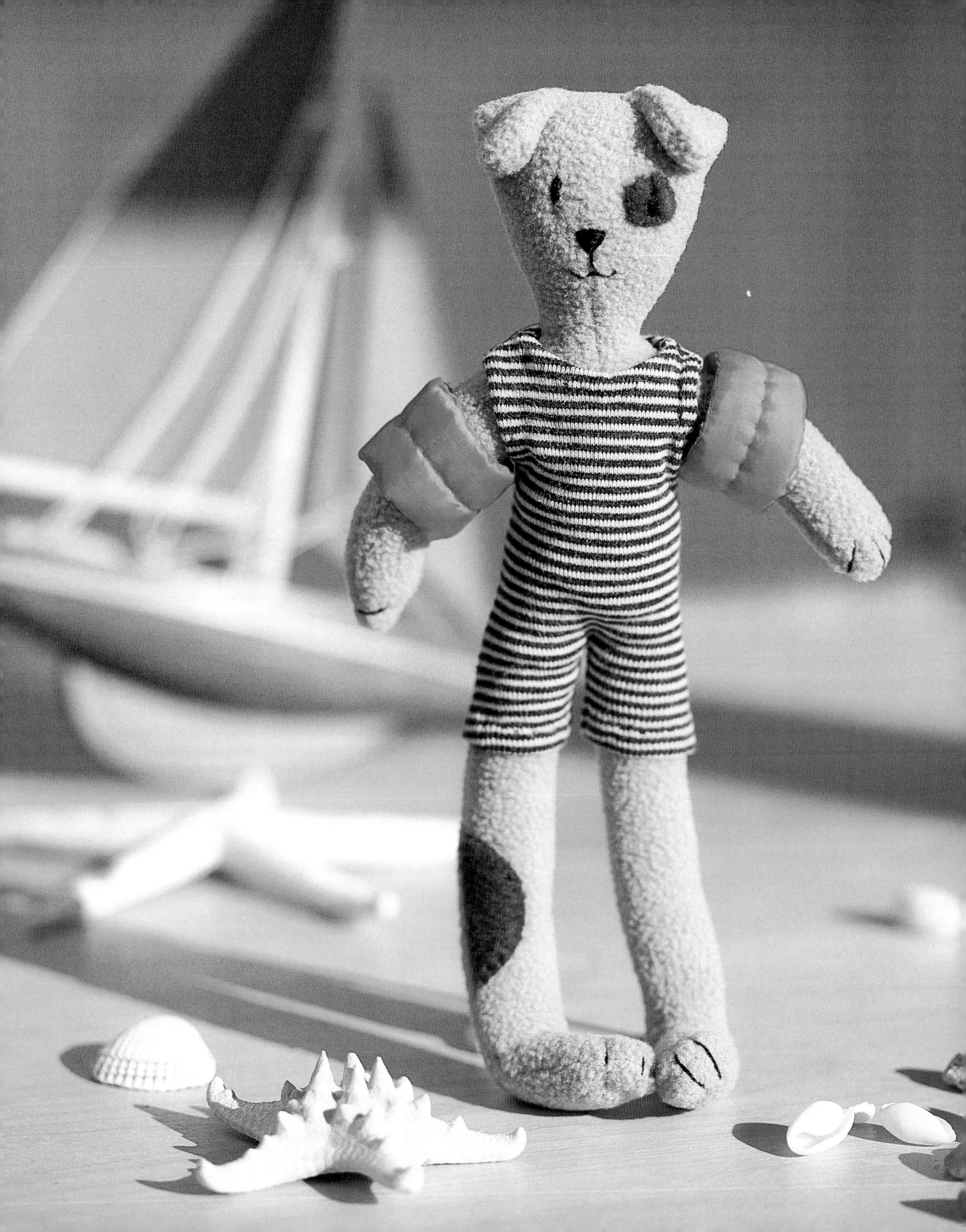

TO MAKE THE DOG

To begin the Dog, see *Starting a Fleecie Pet* (pages 15–17) for complete instructions.

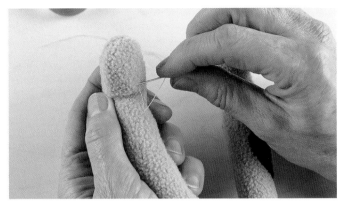

1 Shape the dog's ears by folding them down and securing them in place by working a few small stitches on the underside of the ears, close to the tip. These stitches will be invisible on the finished Fleecie Pet.

2 To shape the dog's feet, turn up 1½ in. (4 cm) at the end of each leg and hold in place so that the foot is at a right angle to the leg. Now, doubling the thread for extra strength and starting at one of the side seams, work several large, loose slip stitches across the curve at the front of the ankle. To make sure that the finished foot is at a right angle to the leg, the slip stitches will need to pick up fabric ¼ in. (7 or 8 mm) on either side of the front ankle crease. Pull the thread fairly tightly and secure.

3 Cut out the eye patch (see page 84 for template) from the dark brown fleece. Position the patch using the photograph as a guide, and topstitch in place. Mark the position of the dog's eyes, nose, and mouth with the water-soluble pen, again using the photograph as a guide. With three strands of black embroidery thread, stitch the eyes by working several ¼-in. (7-mm) vertical stitches in and out of the same holes. For the nose, work a small upside-down triangle in satin stitch. Add the mouth using backstitches.

4 To mark the dog's fingers and toes, use three strands of black embroidery thread. Secure the thread invisibly in the side seam and bring the needle out at the starting point for the base of the first finger or toe. Now bring the thread over the end of the paw, through the back, and then out through the front, ready to form the next finger or toe. Pull the thread fairly tightly so that it stays in position. Work two more fingers or toes in the same way. Finally, secure the thread invisibly in the side seam of the paw.

TO MAKE THE SWIMSUIT AND FLOTATION ARMBANDS

For the swimsuit

1 Photocopy or trace the swimsuit template on page 84 and cut it out. Place the swimsuit template on the cotton jersey, making sure that the stripes run across the width of the swimsuit, and cut out two pieces. Mark the position of the small dots along both sides with the water-soluble pen. Sew the shoulders of the swimsuit, allowing a 1/4-in. (5-mm) seam allowance. Then sew the crotch seam and the side seams up to the small dots.

2 Roll over the raw edge around the neck hole and slip stitch in place on the inside. Do the same around the armholes and leg openings.

For the flotation armbands

1 Fold the orange fabric in half widthwise with right sides facing so that the two short sides meet. Seam along the shorter side 1/4 in. (5 mm) from the outside edge.

2 Turn under 1/4 in. (5 mm) of both raw edges and press in place firmly using your fingers or nails to mark the crease. Bring the raw edges together so that you have a shape a little like a jelly ring mold, with the right side of the fabric on the outside. Stuff lightly with polyester fiber and slip stitch the raw edges together. You may find it easier to slip stitch part of the way around before stuffing. Sew a line of small running stitches around the middle of each armband.

Sniffy the Mouse

Everyone knows that white mice make great pets, and Sniffy is no exception. Her eyes are worked slightly smaller and closer together than most Fleecie Pets' to give them a cute "beady" look. Her flowery skirt and heart-design sweater combine to give her a contemporary country feel. Best of all, she won't ever frighten a living soul.

MATERIALS

For the mouse

- 2 pieces of white fleece, each measuring 9 x 13 in. (22 x 34 cm) (if the fleece has an obvious pile, this should run down the longer length of the fabric)
- Matching colored thread
- $1/2$–$3/4$ oz. (15–20 g) polyester fiber
- Black embroidery thread

For the clothes

- Small amount (approximately $1/2$ oz./15 g) of lime green sport weight yarn for the sweater
- Length of bright pink sport weight yarn for the sweater heart design
- Piece of printed floral cotton or cotton blend fabric for the skirt, measuring $5^{1}/_4$ x 12 in. (13 x 30 cm) (if your fabric has an obvious direction, the pattern should run down the shorter length of the fabric)
- Matching colored thread
- 7 in. (17 cm) white elastic cord for the waistband of the skirt

TOOLS

- Access to a photocopier or a sheet of tracing paper and pencil
- Scissors
- Adhesive tape
- Dressmakers' pins
- Water-soluble pen or quilter's pencil
- Sewing machine (optional)
- Sewing needle
- Embroidery needle
- Pair of size 5 (3.75 mm) knitting needles
- 4 row markers or small safety pins for knitting
- Tapestry needle
- Small safety pin for threading the elastic cord
- Iron

TO MAKE THE MOUSE

To begin the Mouse, see *Starting a Fleecie Pet* (pages 15–17) for complete instructions.

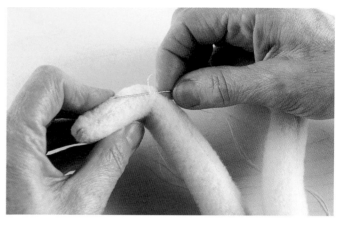

1 Shape the mouse's ears by pinching the base of each ear so that the outer edges are brought forward to form a small pleat. Doubling the thread for extra strength, secure the pleat by handstitching through the base of the ear from the outer side to the inner side and back again. Pull the thread tightly before securing it invisibly in the side seam and trim closely.

2 To shape the feet, turn up 2 in. (5 cm) at the end of each leg and hold in place so that the foot is at a right angle to the leg. Now, doubling the thread for extra strength and starting at one of the side seams, work several large, loose slip stitches across the curve at the front of the ankle. To make sure that the finished foot is at a right angle to the leg, the slip stitches will need to pick up fabric ¼ in. (7 or 8 mm) on either side of the front ankle crease. Pull the thread fairly tightly and secure.

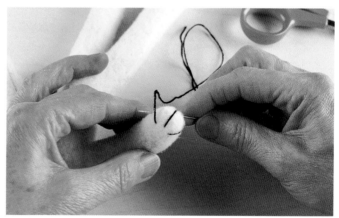

3 Mark the position of the eyes, nose, and mouth with the water-soluble pen, using the photograph as a guide. The eyes should be about ½ in. (1.25 cm) apart. With three strands of black embroidery thread, stitch the eyes by working several ¼-in. (5-mm) vertical stitches in and out of the same holes. For the nose, work a small horizontal rectangle in satin stitch. Add the mouth using backstitches. With a single strand of embroidery thread, sew three whiskers on each cheek.

4 To mark the fingers and toes, use three strands of black embroidery thread. Secure the thread invisibly in the side seam and bring the needle out at the starting point for the base of the first finger or toe. Now bring the thread over the end of the paw, through the back, and then out through the front, ready to form the next finger or toe. Pull the thread fairly tightly so that it stays in position. Work two more fingers or toes in the same way. Finally, secure the thread invisibly in the side seam of the paw.

TO MAKE THE SWEATER AND SKIRT
For the sweater

Abbreviations: see page 13.

Gauge: 10 sts and 12 rows to 1½ in. (4 cm) swatch in st st. If your gauge is noticeably tighter or looser, try using needles that are one size larger or smaller.

Note: When working the heart design, twist the green and pink yarns around each other when you are changing color, on the wrong side of the work, to avoid any holes.

Front
Cast on 19 sts in green. K 4 rows. Beg with a k row, work 4 rows in st st.
Next row k 9. Join pink yarn and k1. Pick up green yarn and k to end.
Next row p 8 green, p 3 pink, p green to end.
Next row k 8 green, k 3 pink, k green to end. Mark beg and end of this row with a row marker or small safety pin (this will be your guide to sewing on the sleeves).
Next row p 7 green, p 5 pink, p green to end.
Next row k 7 green, k 5 pink, k green to end.
Next row p 6 green, p 7 pink, p green to end.
Next row k 6 green, k 7 pink, k green to end.

Next row p 6 green, p 7 pink, p green to end.
Next row k 6 green, k 3 pink, k 1 green, k 3 pink, k green to end.
Next row p 7 green, p 1 pink, p 3 green, p 1 pink, p green to end.
Continue in st st in green only for another 4 rows, ending with a p row.
To shape shoulders, bind off 4 sts at beg of next 2 rows. Continue in st st on remaining 11 sts and work 6 rows, ending with a p row.
Bind off loosely.

Back
Work as for front, but omit heart design. Mark each end of 7th row of st st with a row marker or small safety pin.

Sleeves (make 2)
Cast on 19 sts. K 4 rows. Beg with a k row, work 12 rows in st st. Bind off loosely.

To Finish
Using the tapestry needle, join shoulder seams and side seams of neck. Sew top edge of sleeves to sweater, between row markers. Now stitch sleeve and side seams. For more information on finishing, see page 12.

TIP If you leave long tails of yarn when you cast on and bind off–6-8 in. (15-20 cm) is ideal–you will have plenty of yarn to sew the sweater together and will save yourself time sewing in loose ends.

For the skirt

1 Fold the piece of printed floral cotton in half widthwise, with right sides facing, so that the two short sides meet. Now sew the back seam of the skirt, allowing a ¹/₄-in. (5-mm) seam allowance. Press the seam open with the iron. Turn up ¹/₄ in. (5 mm) at the raw edge of the skirt hem. Press in place. Turn up another ¹/₄ in. (5 mm) and press again. Stitch close to the folded edge—use a machine running stitch if sewing by machine, or a small slipstitch if sewing by hand.

2 To make the waistband, turn down ¹/₄ in. (5 mm) at the top raw edge and press in place. Turn down another ¹/₄ in. (5 mm) and press again. Stitch as close as possible to the folded edge, leaving a ³/₈-in. (1-cm) gap at the back of the skirt for threading the elastic cord. Using the small safety pin, thread the elastic cord through the waistband casing. Knot the ends of the elastic together tightly and trim.

Idea To make a country-style brother for Sniffy, make another mouse and dress him in checkered pants (see page 45 for pants instructions) rather than a floral skirt. An outfit in shades of red and medium-blue would be perfect.

Squealy the Piglet

Made in the softest pale pink fleece, Squealy has no interest whatever in wallowing in the mud and getting dirty. And unlike some of her pigpen mates, she believes in watching her weight so she can show off her new bikini. Squealy's eyes are more widely spaced and higher up than most Fleecie Pets, which give them an endearing piggy look that will delight any fan of these intelligent farmyard favorites.

MATERIALS

For the piglet
- 2 pieces of pale pink fleece, each measuring 9 x 13 in. (22 x 34 cm) (if the fleece has an obvious pile, this should run down the longer length of the fabric)
- Matching colored thread
- $1/2$–$3/4$ oz. (15–20 g) polyester fiber
- Dark gray embroidery thread

For the bikini
- Piece of printed cotton or cotton blend fabric, measuring 6 x 12 in. (15 x 30 cm) (a small print such as the printed floral fabric used here is ideal)
- 6-in. (2 x 15-cm) lengths of narrow ribbon for the bikini straps
- Small amount of contrasting ribbon for the bow on the bikini top (or a small ready-made bow)
- 7 in. (17 cm) white elastic cord for the waistband of the bikini bottom
- Matching colored thread

TOOLS
- Access to a photocopier or a sheet of tracing paper and pencil
- Scissors
- Adhesive tape
- Dressmakers' pins
- Water-soluble pen or quilter's pencil
- Sewing machine (optional)
- Sewing needle
- Embroidery needle
- Small safety pin for threading the elastic cord
- Iron

TO MAKE THE PIGLET

To begin the Piglet, see *Starting a Fleecie Pet* (pages 15–17) for full instructions.

1 Shape the piglet's ears by folding them down and pulling them slightly outward, away from the face. Secure the ears in place by working a few small stitches on the underside of each ear, close to the tip. These stitches will be invisible on the finished Fleecie Pet.

2 To shape the trotters, turn up 1¼ in. (3 cm) at the end of each leg and hold in place so that the foot is at a right angle to the leg. Now, doubling the thread for strength and starting at one of the side seams, work several large, loose slip stitches across the curve at the front of the ankle. To make sure that the finished trotter is at a right angle to the leg, the slip stitches will need to pick up fabric ¼ in. (7 or 8 mm) on either side of the front ankle crease. Pull the thread fairly tightly and secure.

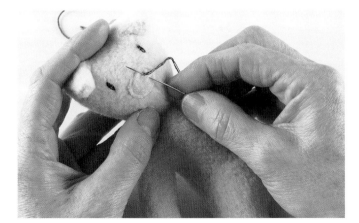

3 Mark the position of the eyes, nose, and mouth with the water-soluble pen, using the photograph as a guide. The eyes should be just below the ears and about 1 in. (2.5 cm) apart. With three strands of dark gray embroidery thread, stitch the eyes by working several ¼-in. (8-mm) vertical stitches in and out of the same holes. For the nose, work a few tiny vertical stitches in and out of the same holes—or you may prefer to use a French knot (see page 11). Add the mouth using backstitches.

4 To mark the piglet's toes, use three strands of dark gray embroidery thread. Secure the thread invisibly in the side seam and bring the needle out at the center of each trotter, about ¼ in. (8 mm) in from the tip. Now bring the thread over the end of the trotter, through the back, and out through the side seam, where you can secure the thread invisibly.

TO MAKE THE BIKINI TOP AND BOTTOM
For the bikini top

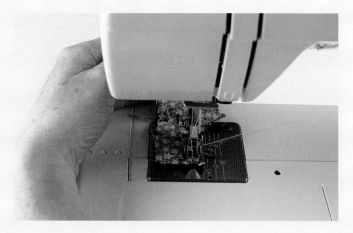

1 Photocopy or trace the bikini top template on page 86 and cut it out. Cut out two identical bikini top pieces from the cotton or cotton blend print fabric. One piece will be the front and the other will be the lining. Pin or baste the two pieces with right sides facing each other and sew along the top edge, 1/4 in. (5 mm) from the outside edge.

2 Open the bikini top out from the bottom edge and, with right sides facing each other, sew the back seam of the bikini top and lining, again allowing a 1/4-in. (5-mm) seam allowance.

3 Trim the tip off the top of the bikini cups close to the seam, and turn the bikini top right side out.
Tie a tight knot at one end of each piece of the bikini strap ribbon and, from the inside, thread through the top of each bikini cup. Turn up 1/4 in. (5 mm) along the raw edges and slip stitch the bikini top and lining together. Make the small bow and stitch it to the center of the bikini top.

Tip If making the bikini top looks like too much work, you could make a quick halter top with ribbon instead. Simply seam down the shorter length of a 5-in. (12.5-cm) piece of 2-in. (5-cm) wide ribbon. Fold the circle of ribbon in half so the raw edges of the seam are on the inside, and slip stitch the long edges together. To finish, tie a single length of narrow ribbon around the center of the bikini top to form two equal-length straps.

For the bikini bottom

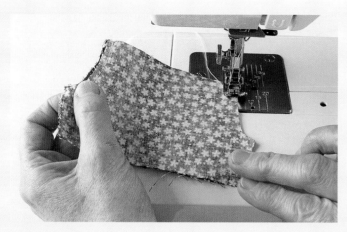

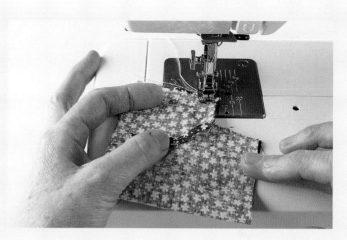

1 Photocopy or trace the bikini bottom template on page 86 and cut it out. Cut out two pieces of cotton or cotton blend fabric for the bikini bottom. With right sides of the fabric facing each other, stitch the crotch seams, allowing a ¼-in. (5-mm) seam allowance. Press the seams open with the iron.

2 Keeping the right sides of the fabric facing each other, match front and back crotch seams, then stitch inside leg seams, again allowing a ¼-in. (5-mm) seam allowance. Press the seams open. Turn up ¼ in. (5 mm) at the raw edge of each leg hem and press in place. Turn up another ¼ in. (5 mm) and press again. Stitch close to the folded edge using a machine running stitch if sewing by machine, or a small slip stitch if sewing by hand.

3 To make the waistband, turn down ¼ in. (5 mm) at the top raw edge and press in place. Turn down another ¼ in. (5 mm) and press again. Stitch as close as possible to the folded edge, leaving a ³⁄₈-in. (1-cm) gap at the back of the bikini bottom for threading the elastic cord. Using the small safety pin, thread the elastic cord through the waistband casing. Knot the ends of the elastic together tightly and trim.

Bruce the Koala

Bruce is much more energetic than the average koala and wants a more interesting life than hanging around in trees, munching eucalyptus leaves. With his colorful shorts and zany top, he's ready to spend his day surfing the ocean waves and posing on the beach. He would make a perfect companion for girl koalas and koala lovers the world over.

MATERIALS

For the koala
- 2 pieces of brown-gray fleece, each measuring 9 x 13 in. (22 x 34 cm) (if the fleece has an obvious pile, this should run down the longer length of the fabric)
- Matching colored thread
- 1/2–3/4 oz. (15–20 g) polyester fiber
- Black embroidery thread

For the clothes
- Piece of orange fleece for the tank top, measuring 4³/₄ x 8 in. (12 x 20 cm) (if the fleece has an obvious pile, this should run down the shorter length of the fabric)
- Scrap of turquoise fleece for the fish motif
- Piece of printed floral cotton or cotton appliqué fabric for the shorts, measuring 5¹/₂ x 11 in. (14 x 28 cm) (if the fabric has an obvious direction, the pattern should run down the shorter length of the fabric)
- Matching colored threads
- Tiny button for the fish's eye
- 7 in. (17 cm) white elastic cord for the waistband of the shorts

TOOLS

- Access to a photocopier or a sheet of tracing paper
- Pencil
- Scissors
- Adhesive tape
- Dressmakers' pins
- Water-soluble pen or quilter's pencil
- Sewing machine (optional)
- Sewing needle
- Embroidery needle
- Small safety pin for threading the elastic cord
- Iron

TO MAKE THE KOALA

To begin the Koala, see *Starting a Fleecie Pet* (pages 15–17) for complete instructions.

1 Shape the koala's ears by sewing a small line of running stitches across the base of the ear on the front side, doubling the thread for extra strength. Pull the thread so the fabric is slightly gathered before securing it invisibly in the side seam, then trim closely.

2 To shape the feet, turn up 1½ in. (3.5 cm) at the end of each leg and hold in place so that the foot is at a right angle to the leg. Now, doubling the thread for strength and starting at one of the side seams, work several large, loose slip stitches across the curve at the front of the ankle. To make sure that the finished foot is at a right angle to the leg, the slip stitches will need to pick up fabric ¼ in. (7 or 8 mm) on either side of the front ankle crease. Pull the thread fairly tightly and secure.

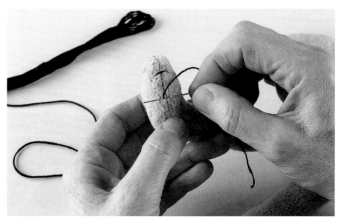

3 Mark the position of the koala's eyes, nose, and mouth with the water-soluble pen, using the photograph as a guide. The eyes should be about ¾ in. (2 cm) apart. With three strands of black embroidery thread, stitch the eyes by working several ¼-in (5-mm) vertical stitches in and out of the same holes. For the nose, work a vertical rectangle in satin stitch. Add the mouth using backstitches.

4 To mark the fingers and toes, use three strands of black embroidery thread. Secure the thread invisibly in the side seam and bring the needle out at the starting point for the base of the first finger or toe. Now bring the thread over the end of the paw, through the back, and then out through the front, ready to form the next finger or toe. Pull the thread fairly tightly so that it stays in position. Work two more fingers or toes in the same way. Secure the thread invisibly in the side seam of the paw.

TO MAKE THE SHORTS AND TANK TOP
For the shorts

1 Photocopy or trace the shorts template on page 87 and cut it out. Cut out two pieces of patterned fabric for the shorts.

2 With right sides of the fabric facing each other, stitch the crotch seams, allowing a 1/4-in. (5-mm) seam allowance. Press the seams open with the iron. Keeping the right sides of the fabric facing each other, match front and back crotch seams then stitch inside leg seams, again allowing a 1/4-in. (5-mm) seam allowance. Press seams open.

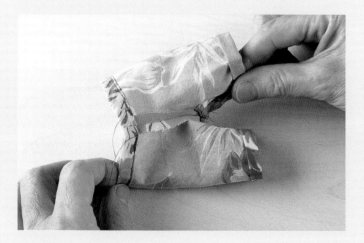

3 To make the waistband, turn down 1/4 in. (5 mm) at the top raw edge and press in place. Turn down another 1/4 in. (5 mm) and press again. Stitch as close as possible to the folded edge, leaving a 3/8-in. (1-cm) gap at the back of the shorts for threading the elastic cord. Using the small safety pin, thread the elastic cord through the waistband casing. Knot the ends of the elastic together tightly and trim. Turn up 1/4 in. (5 mm) at the raw edge of each leg hem and press in place. Turn up another 1/4 in. (5 mm) and press again. Stitch close to the folded edge using a machine running stitch if sewing by machine, or a small slip stitch if sewing by hand.

For the tank top

1 Photocopy or trace the tank top template on page 87 and cut it out. Cut out two tank top front/back pieces from the orange fleece, making sure that any obvious pile runs down the length of the vest. To prepare the fish appliqué, trace the fish shape onto the backing paper of a small piece of fusible webbing using an ordinary lead pencil. Next, with the iron on a warm setting, iron the fusible webbing onto the reverse side of the turquoise fleece. Cut out the fish carefully. Peel off the backing paper and position the appliqué on the front of the tank top as shown on the template. Iron the appliqué in place—you may find it easier to do this by ironing the top on the reverse. Machine or hand stitch around the fish. Sew on the tiny button for the fish's eye.

2 Sew shoulder and side seams of the tank top, allowing a ¼-in. (5-mm) seam allowance. Trim shoulder seam to about ¹⁄₁₆ in. (1 mm) from the stitches (this will help make the finished tank top look neater). Now turn the tank top right side out.

TIP If making an appliqué seems like too much work, take a look in your local notions or craft stores for ready-made appliqués or fish-shaped buttons.

Snowy the Polar Bear Cub

This little polar bear cub is sweet and icy cool. Her pristine pink dress looks sweet against her soft white fur and her favorite pastime is posing and looking pretty while the other animals do the work. She would be a great choice of Fleecie Pet for any little girl who loves teddy bears and all things pink.

MATERIALS

For the bear
- 2 pieces of white fleece, each measuring 9 x 13 in. (22 x 34 cm) (if the fleece has an obvious pile, this should run down the longer length of the fabric)
- Matching colored thread
- $^1/_2$–$^3/_4$ oz. (15–20 g) polyester fiber
- Dark gray embroidery thread

For the clothes
- A piece of bright pink fleece fabric, measuring $6^1/_4$ x $10^1/_4$ in. (16 x 26 cm) (if the fleece has an obvious pile, this should run down the shorter length of the fabric)
- Small piece of pale pink fleece for heart appliqué
- Small piece of fusible webbing
- Matching colored threads

TOOLS
- Access to a photocopier or a sheet of tracing paper
- Pencil
- Scissors
- Adhesive tape
- Dressmakers' pins
- Water-soluble pen or quilter's pencil
- Sewing machine (optional)
- Sewing needle
- Embroidery needle
- Iron

TO MAKE THE POLAR BEAR CUB
To begin the Polar Bear cub, see *Starting a Fleecie Pet* (pages 15–17) for complete instructions.

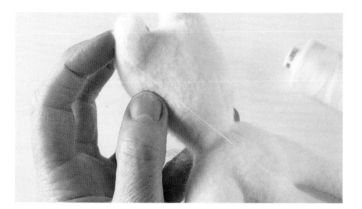

1 To define the ears, work a stitch that looks like an upside down V. Doubling the thread, secure it invisibly in the side seam right by the ear. Bring the needle out through the base of the front of the ear, about $^1/_{12}$ in. (2 mm) from the outer edge. Then bring the needle down through the fabric at the center, right near the tip of the ear. Pick up a tiny amount of fabric at the back of the ear before bringing the needle out to the front again in almost the same place. Bring the thread through the lower part of the ear, just in from the inside edge. Pull the thread very tightly to give the ears a slight curve and secure.

2 To shape the bear cub's feet, turn up 1$^1/_4$ in. (3 cm) at the end of each leg and hold in place so that the foot is at a right angle to the leg. Now, doubling the thread for extra strength and starting at one of the side seams, work several large, loose slip stitches across the curve at the front of the ankle. To make sure that the finished foot is at a right angle to the leg, the slip stitches will need to pick up fabric $^1/_4$ in. (7 or 8 mm) on either side of the front ankle crease. Pull the thread fairly tightly and secure.

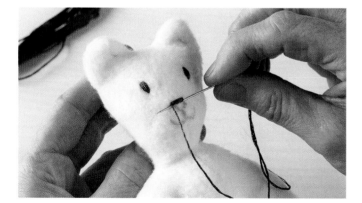

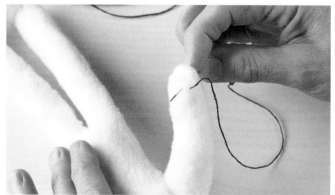

3 Mark the position of the bear cub's eyes, nose, and mouth with the water-soluble pen, using the photograph as a guide. The eyes should be about $^3/_4$ in. (2 cm) apart. With three strands of dark gray embroidery thread, stitch the eyes by working several $^1/_4$-in. (5-mm) vertical stitches in and out of the same holes. For the nose, work a small upside-down triangle in satin stitch. Add the mouth using backstitches.

4 To mark the fingers and toes, use three strands of dark gray embroidery thread. Secure the thread invisibly in the side seam and bring the needle out at the starting point for the base of the first finger or toe. Now bring the thread over the end of the paw, through the back, and then out through the front, ready to form the next finger or toe. Pull the thread fairly tightly so that it stays in position. Work two more fingers or toes in the same way. Finally, secure the thread invisibly in the side seam of the paw.

To make the dress

1 Photocopy or trace the dress template on page 88 and cut it out. Cut out two dress front/back pieces from the bright pink fleece, making sure that any obvious pile runs down the length of the dress.

OPTIONAL EXTRA

If you are using a sewing machine to make the clothes, machine stitch around the finished neck opening using a small zigzag stitch. Do the same around the bottom of the dress, stretching the material slightly as you go. This gives a really nice finish, but it's not essential.

2 To prepare the heart appliqué, trace the heart shape onto the backing paper of a small piece of fusible webbing using an ordinary lead pencil. Next, with the iron on a warm setting, iron the fusible webbing onto the reverse side of the pale pink fleece. Cut out the heart carefully. Peel off the backing paper and position the appliqué on the front of the dress as shown on the template. Iron the appliqué in place—you may find it easier to do this by ironing the dress on the reverse. Machine or hand stitch around the heart.

3 Sew shoulder and side seams of the dress, allowing a 1/4-in. (5-mm) seam allowance. Trim shoulder seam to about 1/16 in. (1 mm) from the stitches (this will help make the finished dress look neater). Now turn the dress right side out.

Tip If making an appliqué seems like too much work, take a look in your local notions or craft stores for ready-made appliqués or heart-shaped buttons.

Hoppy the Rabbit

This rabbit was the first Fleecie Pet I ever made and was inspired by the beautiful cotton Shaker and American folk art rabbits. Hoppy is more contemporarily dressed than her ancestors, but I'm sure she will be just as popular. There's something comforting about a soft rabbit, and she will make a welcome addition to a nursery or young child's bedroom.

MATERIALS

For the rabbit
- 2 pieces of pale gray fleece, each measuring 9 x 15 in. (22 x 38 cm) (if the fleece has an obvious pile, this should run down the longer length of the fabric)
- Matching colored thread
- $1/2$–$3/4$ oz. (15–20 g) polyester fiber
- Black embroidery thread

For the clothes
- Piece of yellow fleece for the tunic top, measuring $5^1/_4$ x 9 in. (13 x 22 cm) (if your fleece has an obvious pile, this should run down the shorter length of the fabric)
- A scrap of coordinating cotton or cotton blend fabric for the flower appliqué
- A small amount of fusible webbing to fasten the appliqué
- A small button for the flower center
- Piece of striped cotton or cotton blend fabric for the pants, measuring 8 x 12 in. (20 x 30 cm) (the stripe should run down the shorter length of the fabric)
- Matching colored threads
- 7 in. (17 cm) white elastic cord for the waistband of the pants

TOOLS
- Access to a photocopier or a sheet of tracing paper
- Pencil
- Scissors
- Adhesive tape
- Dressmakers' pins
- Water-soluble pen or quilter's pencil
- Sewing machine (optional)
- Sewing needle
- Embroidery needle
- Small safety pin for threading the elastic cord
- Iron

TO MAKE THE RABBIT

To begin the Rabbit, see *Starting a Fleecie Pet* (pages 15-17) for complete instructions.

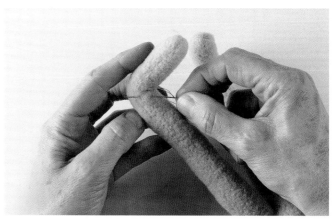

1 Shape the rabbit's ears by pinching the base of each ear so that the outer edges are brought forward to form a small pleat. Doubling the thread for extra strength, secure the pleat by hand, stitching through the base of the ear from the outer side to the inner side and back again. Pull the thread tightly before securing it invisibly in the side seam and trim closely.

2 To shape the feet, turn up 2 in. (5 cm) at the end of each leg and hold in place so that the foot is at a right angle to the leg. Now, doubling the thread for extra strength and starting at one of the side seams, work several large, loose slip stitches across the curve at the front of the ankle. To make sure that the finished foot is at a right angle to the leg, the slip stitches will need to pick up fabric 1/4 in. (7 or 8 mm) on either side of the front ankle crease. Pull the thread fairly tightly and secure.

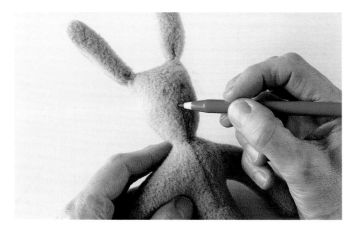

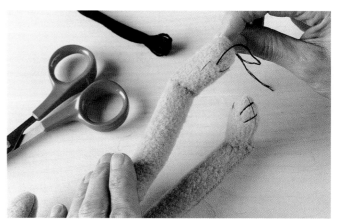

3 Mark the position of the rabbit's eyes, nose, and mouth with the water-soluble pen, using the photograph as a guide. The eyes should be about 3/4 in. (2 cm) apart. With three strands of black embroidery thread, stitch the eyes by working several 1/4-in. (7-mm) vertical stitches in and out of the same holes. For the nose, work a small upside-down triangle in satin stitch. Add the mouth using backstitches.

4 To mark the fingers and toes, use three strands of black embroidery thread. Secure the thread invisibly in the side seam and bring the needle out at the starting point for the base of the first finger or toe. Now bring the thread over the end of the paw, through the back, and then out through the front, ready to form the next finger or toe. Pull the thread fairly tightly so that it stays in position. Work two more fingers or toes in the same way. Finally, secure the thread invisibly in the side seam of the paw.

TO MAKE THE TUNIC TOP AND THE PANTS
For the tunic top

OPTIONAL EXTRA

If you are using a sewing machine to make Hoppy's clothes, machine stitch around the finished neck opening using a small zigzag stitch. Do the same around the bottom of the tunic top, stretching the material slightly as you go. This gives a really nice finish, but it's not essential.

1 Photocopy or trace the tunic top template on page 89 and cut it out. Cut out two tunic top front/back pieces from the yellow fleece, making sure that any obvious pile runs down the length of the top. To prepare the flower appliqué, trace the flower shape onto the backing paper of a small piece of fusible webbing using an ordinary lead pencil. Next, with the iron on a warm setting, iron the fusible webbing onto the reverse side of the appliqué material. Cut out the flower carefully.

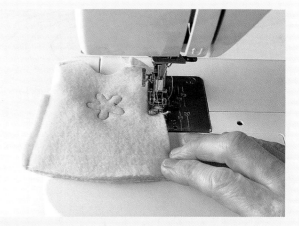

2 Peel off the backing paper and position the appliqué on the front of the tunic top as indicated on the template. Iron the appliqué in place. Machine or hand stitch around the flower. Sew on the button for the flower center.

3 Sew shoulder and side seams of the tunic top, allowing a 1/4-in. (5-mm) seam allowance. Trim shoulder seam to about 1/16 in. (1 mm) from the stitches (this will help make the finished tunic top look neater). Now turn the tunic top right side out.

For the pants

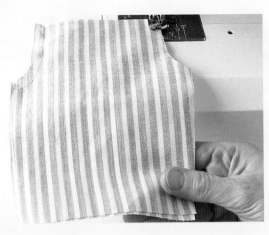

1 Photocopy or trace the pants template on page 91 and cut it out. Cut out two pieces of striped fabric for the pants, making sure that the stripe runs down the length of the pants pieces. With right sides of the fabric facing each other, stitch the crotch seams, allowing a ¼-in. (5-mm) seam allowance. Press the seams open with the iron.

2 Keeping the right sides of the fabric facing each other, match front and back crotch seams, then stitch inside leg seams, again allowing a ¼-in. (5-mm) seam allowance. Press seams open.

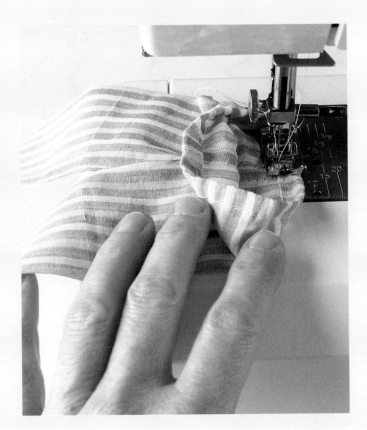

3 Turn up ¼ in. (5 mm) at the raw edge of each leg hem and press in place. Turn up another ¼ in. (5 mm) and press again. Stitch close to the folded edge using a machine running stitch if sewing by machine, or a small slip stitch if sewing by hand. To make the waistband, turn down ¼ in. (5 mm) at the top raw edge and press in place. Turn down another ¼ in. (5 mm) and press again. Stitch as close as possible to the folded edge, leaving a ⅜-in. (1-cm) gap at the back of the pants for threading the elastic cord. Using the small safety pin, thread the elastic cord through the waistband casing. Knot the ends of the elastic together tightly and trim.

Tip If making an appliqué seems like too much work, take a look in your local notions or craft stores for ready-made appliqués or flower-shaped buttons.

Joe the Monkey

Monkeys have been favorite toys for decades, and this little primate with his impish grin should delight any monkey fan. His red polka dot pants give him a hint of 1950s nostalgia, and his starry sweatshirt brings him right up to date. He's more than ready to swing in the jungle, or just stand on a bedroom shelf and look cute.

MATERIALS

For the monkey

- 2 pieces of dark brown fleece, each measuring 9 x 13 in. (22 x 34 cm) (if the fleece has an obvious pile, this should run down the longer length of the fabric)
- Small piece of beige fleece for the monkey's face, measuring $2^1/_2$ x $2^1/_2$ in. (6 x 6 cm)
- Matching colored threads
- $^1/_2$–$^3/_4$ oz. (15–20 g) polyester fiber
- Dark brown embroidery thread

For the clothes

- Piece of turquoise fleece for sweatshirt, measuring 6 x 13 in. (15 x 34 cm) (if the fleece has an obvious pile, this should run down the shorter length of the fabric)
- Small piece of yellow fleece for star appliqué
- Small piece of fusible webbing
- Piece of red polka dot cotton or cotton blend fabric for the pants, measuring 8 x 12 in. (20 x 30 cm)
- Matching colored threads
- 7 in. (17 cm) white elastic cord for the waistband of the pants

TOOLS

- Access to a photocopier or a sheet of tracing paper
- Pencil
- Scissors
- Adhesive tape
- Dressmakers' pins
- Water-soluble pen or quilter's pencil
- Sewing machine (optional)
- Sewing needle
- Embroidery needle
- Small safety pin for threading the elastic cord
- Iron

TO MAKE THE MONKEY

To begin the Monkey, see *Starting a Fleecie Pet* (pages 15–17) for complete instructions.

1   To define the ears, work a stitch that looks like a sideways V. Doubling the thread, secure it invisibly in the side seam just below the ear. Bring the needle out through the inside edge of the front of the ear, about $^1/_{12}$ in. (2 mm) from the bottom. Then bring the needle down through the center of the ear, about $^1/_{12}$ in. (2 mm) from the outer edge. Pick up a tiny amount of fabric at the back of the ear before bringing the needle out to the front again in almost the same place. Bring the thread through the upper inside edge of the ear. Pull the thread very tightly to give the ears a slight curve and secure.

2   To shape the feet, turn up 2 in. (5 cm) at the end of each leg and hold in place so that the foot is at a right angle to the leg. Now, doubling the thread and starting at one of the side seams, work several large, loose slip stitches across the curve at the front of the ankle. To make sure that the finished foot is at a right angle to the leg, the slip stitches will need to pick up fabric $^1/_4$ in. (7 or 8 mm) on either side of the front ankle crease. Pull the thread fairly tightly and secure.

3   Mark the position of the monkey's eyes, nose, and mouth with the water-soluble pen, using the photograph as a guide. The eyes should be more widely set than for most of the other Fleecie Pets—about 1 in. (2.5 cm) apart is ideal. With three strands of dark brown embroidery thread, stitch the eyes by working several $^1/_4$-in. (8-mm) vertical stitches in and out of the same holes. For the nose, work two French knots (see page 11). Add the mouth using backstitches.

4   To mark the fingers and toes, use three strands of dark brown embroidery thread. Secure the thread invisibly in the side seam and bring the needle out at the starting point about $^3/_4$ in. (1.5 cm) from the end of the foot. Bring the thread over the end of the foot, through the back, and then out through the front, ready to form the next finger or toe. Pull the thread fairly tightly so that it stays in position. Work two more fingers or toes in the same way. Finally, secure the thread invisibly in the side seam.

TO MAKE THE SWEATSHIRT AND THE PANTS
For the sweatshirt

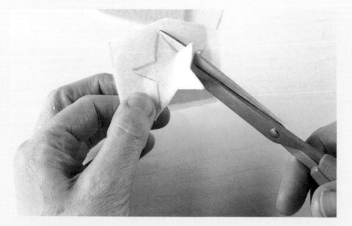

1 Photocopy or trace the sweatshirt templates on pages 89–90 and cut them out. Cut out two sweatshirt front/back pieces and two sleeve pieces from the turquoise fleece, making sure that any obvious pile runs down the length of the top and sleeves. For the star, trace the shape onto the backing paper of a piece of fusible webbing using an ordinary lead pencil. Next, with the iron on a warm setting, iron the fusible webbing onto the reverse side of the piece of yellow fleece. Cut out the star carefully.

2 Peel off the backing paper and position the appliqué on the front of the sweatshirt, as shown on the template. Iron the appliqué in place—you may find it easier to do this by ironing the top on the reverse side. Machine or hand stitch around the star.

3 Sew shoulder seams of sweatshirt allowing a ¼-in. (5-mm) seam allowance. Position sleeves between small dots, making sure that any obvious pile runs down the length of the sleeve, and stitch in place. Then sew the sleeve and side seams. Now turn the sweatshirt right side out.

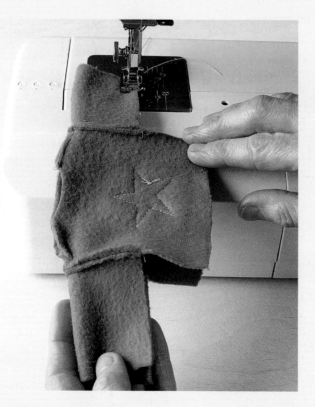

OPTIONAL EXTRA

If you are using a sewing machine to make Joe's clothes, machine stitch around the finished bottom of the sweatshirt using a small zigzag stitch. This gives a really nice finish, but it's not essential.

For the pants

1 Photocopy or trace the pants template on page 91 and cut it out. Cut out two pieces of polka dot fabric for the pants. With right sides of the fabric facing each other, stitch the crotch seams, allowing a ¼-in. (5-mm) seam allowance. Press the seams open with the iron.

2 Keeping the right sides of the fabric facing each other, match front and back crotch seams, then stitch inside leg seams, again allowing a ¼-in. (5-mm) seam allowance. Press seams open.

3 Turn up ¼ in. (5 mm) at the raw edge of each leg hem and press in place. Turn up another ¼ in. (5 mm) and press again. Stitch close to the folded edge using a machine running stitch if sewing by machine, or a small slip stitch if sewing by hand. To make the waistband, turn down ¼ in. (5 mm) at the top raw edge and press in place. Turn down another ¼ in. (5 mm) and press again. Stitch as close as possible to the folded edge, leaving a ³⁄₈-in. (1-cm) gap at the back of the pants for threading the elastic cord. Using the small safety pin, thread the elastic cord through the waistband casing. Knot the ends of the elastic together tightly and trim.

Tip If making an appliqué seems like too much work, take a look in your local notions or craft stores for ready-made appliqués or star-shaped buttons.

Spangles the Cat

With her slightly haughty air, Spangles considers herself to be a cut above your average family cat. She takes the utmost care with her appearance and her favorite outfit at the moment is this ballet skirt, matching pullover sweater, and girly handbag. She is a must for cat lovers everywhere and solemnly promises not to scratch the upholstery.

MATERIALS

For the cat

- 2 pieces of dark gray fleece, each measuring 9 x 13 in. (22 x 34 cm) (if the fleece has an obvious pile, this should run down the longer length of the fabric)
- Small piece of white fleece for patches
- Matching colored threads
- $1/2$–$3/4$ oz. (15–20 g) polyester fiber
- Black embroidery thread

For the clothes

- Small amount (approximately $1/2$ oz./15 g) of pale pink sport weight yarn for the sweater
- Piece of pale pink polyester netting or tulle (similar to netting but finer) for the tutu, measuring $21^1/2$ x $9^1/2$ in. (55 x 24 cm)
- Piece of pale pink organza for the underskirt, measuring $21^1/2$ x $9^1/2$ in. (55 x 24 cm)
- Matching colored thread
- 2 lengths of white elastic cord, each 7-in. (17-cm) long for the waistbands of the tutu and underskirt
- Small crystal button—$1/4$ in. (9 mm) diameter

For the handbag

- Length of mauve sport weight yarn
- Small mother of pearl button—$1/4$ in. (9 mm) diameter

TOOLS

- Access to a photocopier or a sheet of tracing paper and pencil
- Scissors
- Adhesive tape
- Dressmakers' pins
- Water-soluble pen or quilter's pencil
- Sewing machine (optional)
- Sewing needle
- Embroidery needle
- Pair of size 5 (3.75 mm) knitting needles
- A size 6 (4 mm) crochet hook
- 4 row markers or small safety pins for knitting
- Tapestry needle
- Small safety pin for threading the elastic cord
- Iron

TO MAKE THE CAT

To begin the Cat, see *Starting a Fleecie Pet* (pages 15–17) for complete instructions.

1 To define the ears, work an upside-down V stitch on the front of the ear. Doubling the thread, secure it invisibly in the side seam right by the ear. Bring the needle out through the base of the front of the ear, about 1/12 in. (2 mm) from the outer edge. Then bring the needle down through the fabric at the center of the ear, right near the tip. Pick up a tiny amount of fabric at the back of the ear before bringing your needle out to the front again in almost the same place. Bring your thread through the lower inside edge of the ear. Pull the thread slightly to give the ears a slight curve and secure.

2 To shape the feet, turn up 1 1/2 in. (4 cm) at the end of each leg and hold in place so that the foot is at a right angle to the leg. Now, doubling the thread for extra strength and starting at one of the side seams, work several large, loose slip stitches across the curve at the front of the ankle. To make sure that the finished foot is at a right angle to the leg, the slip stitches will need to pick up fabric 1/4 in. (7 or 8 mm) on either side of the front ankle crease. Pull the thread fairly tightly and secure.

3 Mark the position of the eyes, nose, and mouth with the water-soluble pen, using the photograph as a guide. The eyes should be about 3/4 in. (2 cm) apart. With three strands of black embroidery thread, stitch the eyes by working several 1/4-in. (5-mm) vertical stitches in and out of the same holes. For the nose, work a small upside down triangle in satin stitch. Add the mouth using back stitch. With a single strand of embroidery thread, sew three whiskers on each cheek.

4 To mark the fingers and toes, use three strands of black embroidery thread. Secure the thread invisibly in the side seam and bring the needle out at the starting point for the base of the first finger or toe. Now bring the thread over the end of the paw, through the back, and then out through the front, ready to form the next finger or toe. Pull the thread fairly tightly so that it stays in position. Work two more fingers or toes in the same way. Finally, secure the thread invisibly in the side seam of the paw.

TO MAKE THE TUTU, UNDERSKIRT, SWEATER, AND HANDBAG

For the tutu

1 Fold the piece of netting or tulle in half widthwise, so that the two short sides meet. Now sew the back seam of the skirt, allowing a ¼-in. (5-mm) seam allowance. Press the seam open with your fingers.

2 Bring the raw edges of the tutu together so that your material is double and the back seam is on the inside. To make the waistband, sew a line of stitches around the top folded edge of the skirt, about ⅜ in. (1 cm) from the edge, leaving a ⅜-in. (1-cm) gap at the back of the skirt over the seam for threading the elastic cord. Using the small safety pin, thread the elastic cord through the waistband casing. Knot the ends of the elastic together tightly and trim.

For the underskirt

The underskirt is made in exactly the same way as the tutu except that after step 1 you will need to hem both raw edges. Turn up ¼ in. (5 mm) at edges and press in place using a cool iron. Turn up another ¼ in. (5 mm) at both edges and press again. Stitch close to the folded edges—use a machine running stitch if sewing by machine, or a small slip stitch if sewing by hand. Once you have done this, bring the two hemmed edges together so that the seam is on the inside and make the waistband as for the tutu, as outlined in step 2, above.

For the sweater

Abbreviations: see page 13.

Gauge: 10 sts and 12 rows to 1¹/₂ in. (4 cm) swatch in st st. If your gauge is noticeably tighter or looser, try using needles that are one size larger or smaller.

Front

Cast on 19 sts in pale pink. K 4 rows. Beg with a k row, work 18 rows in st st, marking the beg and end of the 7th row with a row marker or small safety pin (this will be your guide to sewing on the sleeves).
To shape shoulders, bind off 4 sts at beg of next 2 rows. Continue in st st on remaining 11 sts and work 6 rows, ending with a p row.
Bind off loosely.

Back

Work exactly as for front.

Sleeves (make 2)

Cast on 19 sts. K 4 rows. Beg with a k row, work 12 rows in st st. Bind off loosely.

To Finish

Using the tapestry needle, join shoulder seams and side seams of neck. Sew top edge of sleeves to sweater, between row markers. Now stitch sleeve and side seams. For more information on finishing, see page 12. Finish sweater by sewing the crystal button just below the roll collar, as shown in the photograph on page 52.

For the handbag

Note: The handbag is made in one piece, ending with the top flap of the bag, and is worked in garter stitch throughout.

Cast on 11 sts in mauve, leaving a 8-in. (20-cm) tail that will form the handbag handle.
K 2 rows.
Inc 1 st at either end of next and every alt row until there are 17 sts.
Work 13 rows.
Ssk at beg and k2tog at end of next and every alt row until there are 11 sts.
K 7 rows.
Ssk at beg and k2tog at end of next 3 rows.
Bind off remaining 5 sts leaving a long 6-in. (15-cm) tail to use to make button loop.

To Finish

Fold the bottom of the handbag upward and topstitch the sides of bag together using the mauve yarn and tapestry needle. With tail of yarn at bind-off edge, work 5 chain stitches using crochet hook (see page 14 for more information). Pull end of yarn through final chain and secure in place to make button loop. Make bag handle by crocheting a 2¹/₄-in. (5.5-cm) chain from the tail of yarn at the cast-on edge. Pull end of yarn through final chain and stitch free end of handle in place. Complete the handbag by sewing on the button.

> **TIP** If you leave long tails of yarn when you cast on and bind off—6-8 in. (15-20 cm) is ideal—you will have plenty of yarn to sew the sweater together, and will save yourself time sewing in loose ends.

Rumble the Bear

Cuddly bears have been around since the end of the 19th century. They are probably the most loved of all soft toys, and I couldn't complete this collection without at least one. Rumble, in his cheerful red dungarees, is a hardworking, straightforward guy with respect for old-fashioned values. He will make a wonderful addition to teddy bear collections everywhere.

MATERIALS
For the bear
- 2 pieces of beige fleece, each measuring 9 x 13 in. (22 x 34 cm) (if the fleece has an obvious pile, this should run down the longer length of the fabric)
- Matching colored thread
- $^1/_2$–$^3/_4$ oz. (15–20 g) polyester fiber
- Dark brown embroidery thread

For the clothes
- A piece of red finely ribbed corduroy, measuring 10 x 12 in. (25 x 30 cm) (the lines of the corduroy should run down the shorter length of the fabric)
- Matching colored thread
- 2 small snap fasteners
- 2 small white buttons—$^1/_4$ in. (9 mm) diameter

TOOLS
- Access to a photocopier or a sheet of tracing paper and pencil
- Scissors
- Adhesive tape
- Dressmakers' pins
- Water-soluble pen or quilter's pencil
- Sewing machine (optional)
- Sewing needle
- Embroidery needle
- Iron

TO MAKE THE BEAR

To begin the Bear, see *Starting a Fleecie Pet* (pages 15–17) for complete instructions.

1 To define the ears, work a stitch that looks like an upside-down V. Doubling the thread, secure it invisibly in the side seam right by the ear. Bring the needle out through the base of the front of the ear, about ¹/₁₂ in. (2 mm) from the outer edge. Then bring the needle down through the fabric at the center, right near the tip of the ear. Pick up a tiny amount of fabric at the back of the ear before bringing your needle out to the front again in almost the same place. Bring your thread through the lower part of the ear, just in from the inside edge. Pull the thread very tightly to give the ears a slight curve and secure.

2 To shape the bear's feet, turn up 1¼ in. (3 cm) at the end of each leg and hold in place so that the foot is at a right angle to the leg. Now, doubling the thread for extra strength and starting at one of the side seams, work several large, loose slip stitches across the curve at the front of the ankle. To make sure that the finished foot is at a right angle to the leg, the slip stitches will need to pick up fabric ¼ in. (7 or 8 mm) on either side of the front ankle crease. Pull up the thread fairly tightly and secure.

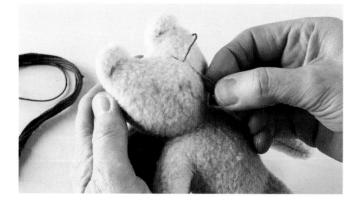

3 Mark the position of the bear's eyes, nose, and mouth with the water-soluble pen, using the photograph as a guide. The eyes should be about ³/₄ in. (2 cm) apart. With three strands of dark brown embroidery thread, stitch the eyes by working several ¹/₄-in. (5-mm) vertical stitches in and out of the same holes. For the nose, work a small upside-down triangle in satin stitch. Add the mouth using backstitches.

4 To mark the fingers and toes, use three strands of dark brown embroidery thread. Secure the thread invisibly in the side seam and bring the needle out at the starting point for the base of the first finger or toe. Now bring the thread over the end of the paw, through the back, and then out through the front, ready to form the next finger or toe. Pull the thread fairly tightly so that it stays in position. Work two more fingers or toes in the same way. Finally, secure the thread invisibly in the side seam.

To make the dungarees

1 Photocopy or trace the templates for the dungarees on page 93 and cut out two leg and bib pieces, two straps and one pocket. Fold in ⅛ in. (3 mm) around pocket edges and press. Sew along the top of the pocket and stitch the pocket in place on the bib, as shown on the template. Place the two bib pieces right sides together and sew around the top and sides, leaving a ¼ in. (5 mm) seam allowance. Turn right sides out. Sew one crotch seam on pants pieces and press open. Pin and baste the bottom edge of the front side of the bib across the top of the crotch seam as shown, and stitch ¼ in. (5 mm) from raw edge. Sew remaining crotch seam and inside leg seams.

2 Turn down ¼ in. (5 mm) around raw edge of waist and iron in place. Sew around entire waist, including bib, using a small zigzag stitch if sewing by machine, or a small slip stitch if sewing by hand. Turn up ¼ in. (5 mm) of the raw edge of each leg and press in place. Turn up another ¼ in. (5 mm) and press again. Stitch close to the folded edge using a machine running stitch if sewing by machine, or a small slip stitch if sewing by hand.

3 For the straps, fold the long outer edges toward the middle of the strap so that they cross over slightly. Stitch along the middle of the strap using a medium zigzag stitch if sewing by machine, or a small running stitch if sewing by hand. Place the two straps at the inside back of the dungarees so that they cross and machine or hand stitch in place along the waistline, as shown. Now you can put the dungarees on your bear to measure where to put the snap fasteners on the strap fronts and reverse side of the bib before sewing on the decorative buttons.

Scrounger the Rat

It's true that rats are not the most loved of creatures, but Scrounger is an exception. With his patched pants and cool bandanna, he's more lovable rogue than pesky rodent, but his piercing gaze lets you know who's boss. Scrounger will be an ideal gift for little boys everywhere who, like this little rat, like nothing better than running around outside and getting dirty.

MATERIALS

For the rat
- 2 pieces of pale brown fleece, each measuring 9 x 13 in. (22 x 34 cm) (if the fleece has an obvious pile, this should run down the longer length of the fabric)
- Matching colored thread
- $^1/_2$–$^3/_4$ oz. (15–20 g) polyester fiber
- Black embroidery thread

For the clothes
- Small amounts (approximately $^1/_2$ oz./10g) of medium blue and cream sport weight yarn for the sweater
- Piece of pale blue chambray or light denim for the pants, measuring 8 x 12 in. (20 x 30 cm)
- Scraps of red plaid fabric for the pants patch and patterned red fabric for the bandanna
- Matching colored thread
- 7 in. (17 cm) white elastic cord for the waistband of the pants

TOOLS
- Access to a photocopier or a sheet of tracing paper and pencil
- Scissors
- Adhesive tape
- Dressmakers' pins
- Water-soluble pen or quilter's pencil
- Sewing machine (optional)
- Sewing needle
- Embroidery needle
- Pair of size 5 (3.75 mm) knitting needles
- 4 row markers or small safety pins for knitting
- Tapestry needle
- Small safety pin for threading the elastic cord
- Iron

TO MAKE THE RAT

To begin the Rat, see *Starting a Fleecie Pet* (pages 15–17) for complete instructions.

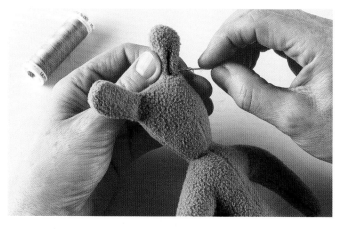

1 Shape the rat's ears by pinching the base of each ear so that the outer edges are brought forward to form a small pleat. Doubling the thread for extra strength, secure the pleat by hand stitching through the base of the ear from the outer side to the inner side and back again. Pull the thread tightly before securing it invisibly in the side seam and trim closely.

2 To shape the feet, turn up 2 in. (5 cm) at the end of each leg and hold in place so that the foot is at a right angle to the leg. Now, doubling the thread for extra strength and starting at one of the side seams, work several large, loose slip stitches across the curve at the front of the ankle. To make sure that the finished foot is at a right angle to the leg, the slip stitches will need to pick up fabric ¼ in. (7 or 8 mm) either side of the front ankle crease. Pull the thread fairly tightly and secure.

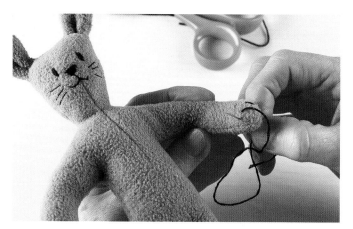

3 Mark the position of the rat's eyes, nose, and mouth with the water-soluble pen, using the photograph as a guide. The eyes should be about ¾ in. (1.5 cm) apart. With three strands of black embroidery thread, stitch the eyes by working several ¼-in. (5-mm) vertical stitches in and out of the same holes. For the nose, work a small upside down triangle in satin stitch. Add the mouth using backstitches. With a single strand of embroidery thread, sew three whiskers on each cheek.

4 To mark the fingers and toes, use three strands of black embroidery thread. Secure the thread invisibly in the side seam and bring the needle out at the starting point for the base of the first finger or toe. Now bring the thread over the end of the paw, through the back, and then out through the front, ready to form the next finger or toe. Pull the thread fairly tightly so that it stays in position. Work two more fingers or toes in the same way. Finally, secure the thread invisibly in the side seam of the paw.

TO MAKE THE SWEATER, PANTS, AND BANDANNA
For the sweater

Abbreviations: see page 13.

Gauge: 10 sts and 12 rows to 1¹/₂ in. (4 cm) swatch in st st. If your gauge is noticeably tighter or looser, try using needles that are one size larger or smaller.

Note: When knitting stripes, you do not need to cut the ends when you have finished each stripe. Simply leave the yarn and bring it up the side of your work when you need it again, taking care not to pull it too tightly.

Front
Cast on 19 sts in blue. K 4 rows.
Change to cream yarn and beg with a k row, work 4 rows in st st.
Rejoin blue yarn and continuing in st st, work 2 rows.
Continuing in st st, mark beg and end of next row with a row marker or small safety pin (this will be your guide to sewing on the sleeves). Work one more row in st st.
Rejoin cream yarn and work another 4 rows in st st.
Rejoin blue yarn and work another 4 rows in st st.

Rejoin cream yarn and work 2 rows in st st. Continuing in cream, shape shoulders by binding off 4 sts at beg of next 2 rows.
Rejoin blue yarn. Continue in st st on remaining 11 sts and work 6 rows, ending with a p row.
Bind off loosely.

Back
Work as for front.

Sleeves (make 2)
Cast on 19 sts in blue. K 4 rows. Change to cream yarn and beg with a k row, work 4 rows in st st. Continue in st st in the blue/cream stripe pattern for another 8 rows. Bind off loosely.

To Finish
Using the tapestry needle, join shoulder seams and side seams of neck. Sew top edge of sleeves to sweater, between row markers. Now stitch sleeve and side seams. For more information on finishing, see page 12.

For the pants

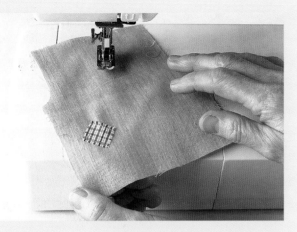

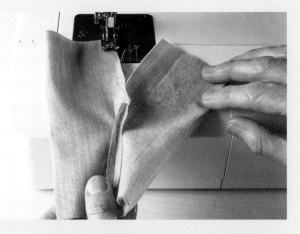

1 Photocopy or trace the pants template on page 91 and cut it out. Scrounger's pants should be shorter than the other Pets', so you may want to adjust the legs accordingly. Cut out two pieces of chambray or denim for the pants. On one of the pants pieces, sew on a ³/₄ in. (2 cm) square of red plaid fabric for the patch, see photograph above for positioning. With right sides of the fabric facing each other, stitch the crotch seams, allowing a ¹/₄-in. (5-mm) seam allowance. Press the seams open with the iron.

2 Keeping the right sides of the fabric facing each other, match front and back crotch seams, then stitch inside leg seams, again allowing a ¹/₄-in. (5-mm) seam allowance. Press seams open.

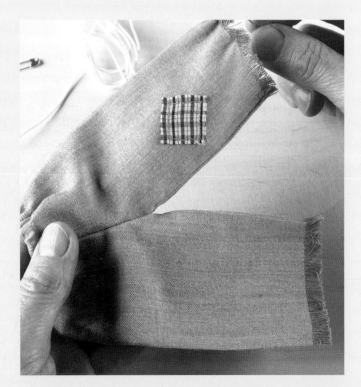

3 To make the waistband, turn down ¹/₄ in. (5 mm) at the top raw edge and press in place. Turn down another ¹/₄ in. (5 mm) and press again. Stitch as close as possible to the folded edge, leaving a ³/₈-in. (1-cm) gap at the back of the pants for threading the elastic cord. Using the small safety pin, thread the elastic cord through the waistband casing. Knot the ends of the elastic together tightly and trim. Using a sewing needle, fray approximately ¹/₄ in. (5 mm) at the lower edges of the pants as shown.

For the bandanna

Cut out a strip of red patterned fabric measuring ³/₄ x 7 in. (2 x 17 cm). Leave the raw edges unfinished and tie loosely around the neck of the finished rat.

Fuzzy the Sheep

This groovy little sheep loves grazing and daydreaming. Her widely set eyes and curly topknot give her a distinctive look. While her funky floral pants and acrylic sheepskin coat hark back to the dreamy days of the 1960s, Fuzzy is the epitome of 21st-century cool and is looking for a like-minded owner.

MATERIALS

For the sheep
- 2 pieces of white fleece, each measuring 9 x 13 in. (22 x 34 cm) (if the fleece has an obvious pile, this should run down the longer length of the fabric)
- Length of cream sport weight yarn
- Matching colored thread
- 1/2–3/4 oz. (15–20 g) polyester fiber
- Dark brown embroidery thread

For the clothes
- Piece of floral cotton or cotton blend fabric for the pants, measuring 8 x 12 in. (20 x 30 cm)
- Piece of acrylic sheepskin jacket lining or fleece for the coat, measuring 7 x 16 1/2 in. (18 x 42 cm)
- Matching colored threads
- 7 in. (17 cm) white elastic cord for the waistband of the pants
- 2 small snap fasteners
- 2 small brown buttons—1/4 in. (9 mm) diameter

TOOLS
- Access to a photocopier or a sheet of tracing paper and pencil
- Scissors
- Adhesive tape
- Dressmakers' pins
- Water-soluble pen or quilter's pencil
- Sewing machine (optional)
- Sewing needle
- Embroidery needle
- Pair of size 5 (3.75 mm) knitting needles
- Small safety pin for threading the elastic cord
- Iron

TO MAKE THE SHEEP

To begin the Sheep, see *Starting a Fleecie Pet* (pages 15–17) for complete instructions.

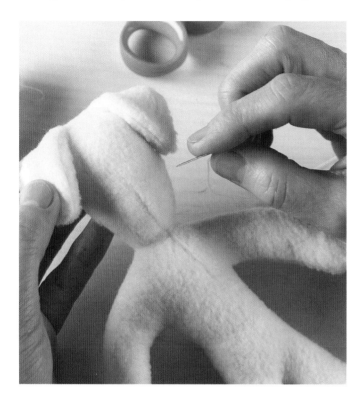

1 Shape the sheep's ears by folding them down and pulling them slightly outward, away from the face. Secure the ears in place by working a few small stitches on the underside of each ear. These stitches will be invisible on the finished Pet.

2 To shape the sheep's feet, turn up 1¹⁄₂ in. (3.5 cm) at the end of each leg and hold in place so that the foot is at a right angle to the leg. Now, doubling the thread for extra strength and starting at one of the side seams, work several large, loose slip stitches across the curve at the front of the ankle. To make sure that the finished foot is at a right angle to the leg, the slip stitches will need to pick up fabric ¹⁄₄ in. (7 or 8 mm) on either side of the front ankle crease. Pull up the thread fairly tightly and secure.

Tip To stitch the sheep's ear invisibly, first hold the ear firmly in position. Still holding the top of the ear firmly, lift the tip of the ear to reveal the underside. Now you can make your stitches.

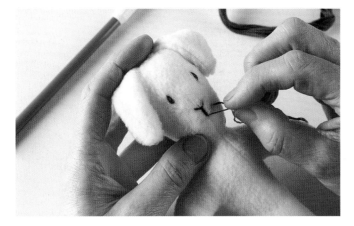

3 Mark the position of the sheep's eyes, nose, and mouth with the water-soluble pen, using the photograph as a guide. The eyes should be slightly higher than for most Fleecie Pets and more widely set— about 1 in. (2.5 cm) apart is ideal. With three strands of dark brown embroidery thread, stitch the eyes by working a few 1/4-in. (5-mm) vertical stitches in and out of the same holes. Work the nose and mouth using back stitches.

4 To mark the sheep's hooves, use three strands of dark brown embroidery thread. Secure the thread invisibly in the side seam and bring the needle out at the center of each hoof, about 1/4 in. (8 mm) from the tip. Now bring the thread over the end of the hoof, through the back, and out through the side seam, where you can secure the thread invisibly.

5 To complete the sheep, make a woolly topknot. Using size 5 (3.75 mm) knitting needles, cast on 10 stitches and knit a few rows in garter stitch. Dampen slightly and leave to dry (this will ensure that the curl stays in when you unravel it). Unravel the yarn and loosely wrap a length of it (approximately 16 in./40 cm) around two fingers. Slip the loops off and join at the center to the top of the sheep's head with matching colored thread.

TO MAKE THE PANTS AND COAT
For the pants

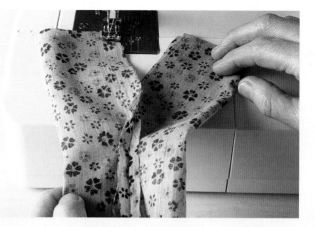

1 Photocopy or trace the pants template on page 91 and cut it out. Cut out two pieces of floral fabric for the pants. With right sides of the fabric facing each other, stitch the crotch seams, allowing a 1/4-in. (5-mm) seam allowance. Press the seams open with the iron.

2 Keeping the right sides of the fabric facing each other, match front and back crotch seams, then stitch inside leg seams, again allowing a 1/4-in. (5-mm) seam allowance. Press seams open.

3 Turn up 1/4 in. (5 mm) at the raw edge of each leg hem and press in place. Turn up another 1/4 in. (5 mm) and press again. Stitch close to the folded edge using a machine running stitch if sewing by machine, or a small slip stitch if sewing by hand. To make the waistband, turn down 1/4 in. (5 mm) at the top raw edge and press in place. Turn down another 1/4 in. (5 mm) and press again. Stitch as close as possible to the folded edge, leaving a 3/8-in. (1-cm) gap at the back of the pants for threading the elastic cord. Using the small safety pin, thread the elastic cord through the waistband casing. Knot the ends of the elastic together tightly and trim.

For the coat

1 Photocopy or trace the coat templates on pages 91–92 and cut them out. Cut out two pockets, one back and two front pieces from the acrylic sheepskin fabric. Remember that the coat has a right and left side, so you will need to cut one front piece using the template right side up and the other using the template facedown. Position the pockets as shown on the template and baste in place using a few large running stitches. Because the fabric is bulky, you will probably find it easier to hand stitch rather than machine stitch the pockets in place around the sides and bottom.

2 With right sides of the fabric together, sew the two fronts of the coat to the back at sleeve and side seams, allowing a ¼-in. (5-mm) seam. Trim the seam allowance to ¹⁄₁₆ in. (1 mm) (this will help make the coat less bulky and give it a better fit). Turn the coat right side out. If you are using a sewing machine to make Fuzzy's clothes, work a small zigzag stitch around the entire outer edge of the coat. This isn't essential, but it gives the coat a more professional finish.

3 Sew the two buttons in place on the right side of the coat, as shown in the photograph on page 66. Overlap the right side of the coat over the left side. Sew one part of the snap fasteners on the inside of the coat, directly underneath the buttons, and the corresponding parts on the top of the left side of the coat.

Leapy the Frog

Even people who run away at the sight of a real frog would be happy to give Leapy a home.

In his bright yellow raincoat, he's prepared for a shower or even a downpour and would

feel quite at home brightening up any bathroom. Best of all, he's not in the least bit slimy.

MATERIALS

For the frog
- 2 pieces of green fleece, each measuring 9 x 13 in. (22 x 34 cm) (if the fleece has an obvious pile, this should run down the longer length of the fabric)
- Matching colored thread
- $1/2$–$3/4$ oz. (15–20 g) polyester fiber
- Black embroidery thread

For the clothes
- A piece of yellow polyester or nylon fabric (such as that used for lightweight raincoats), measuring 10 x 15 in. (25 x 38 cm)
- Matching colored thread

TOOLS
- Access to a photocopier or a sheet of tracing paper and pencil
- Scissors
- Adhesive tape
- Dressmakers' pins
- Water-soluble pen or quilter's pencil
- Sewing machine (optional)
- Sewing needle
- Embroidery needle

TO MAKE THE FROG

To begin the Frog, see *Starting a Fleecie Pet* (pages 15–17) for complete instructions.

1 To shape the frog's feet, turn up 2 in. (5 cm) at the end of each leg and hold in place so that the foot is at a right angle to the leg. Now, doubling the thread for extra strength and starting at one of the side seams, work several large, loose slip stitches across the curve at the front of the ankle. To make sure that the finished foot is at a right angle to the leg, the slip stitches will need to pick up fabric 1/4 in. (7 or 8 mm) on either side of the front ankle crease. Pull the thread fairly tightly and secure.

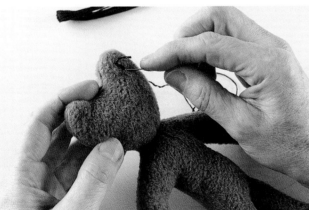

2 Mark the position of the frog's eyes, nose, and mouth with the water-soluble pen, using the photograph as a guide. With three strands of black embroidery thread, stitch the eyes by working several 1/4-in. (5-mm) vertical stitches in and out of the same holes. For the nose, work three or four tiny vertical stitches in and out of the same holes—or you may prefer to use an embroidery stitch called a French knot (see page 11). Add the mouth using backstitches.

3 To mark the frog's fingers and toes, use three strands of the thread you have used to sew the frog (or you can use a matching embroidery thread). The frog's toes should be slightly longer than for most other Fleecie Pets—about 3/4 in. (1.5 cm) is ideal. Secure the thread invisibly in the side seam and bring the needle out at the starting point for the base of the first finger or toe. Now bring the thread over the end of the hand or foot, through the back, and then out through the front, ready to form the next finger or toe. Pull the thread fairly tightly so that it stays in position. Work two more fingers or toes in the same way. Finally, secure the thread invisibly in the side seam.

To make the raincoat

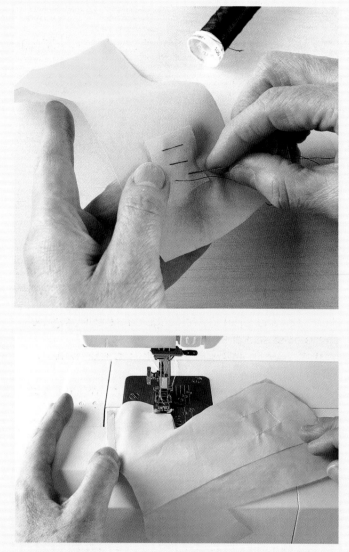

1 Photocopy or trace the raincoat front and back templates on pages 91–92 and cut out one back and two front pieces from the yellow polyester or nylon fabric. Remember that the raincoat has a right and left side, so you will need to cut one front piece using the template right side up and the other using the template facedown. (If the fabric is identical on both sides, you do not have to do this.) Cut out two 3/4 x 1 in. (2 x 2.5 cm) pockets and baste in place on the coat fronts, as shown on the template, using a few large running stitches. Machine or hand stitch around the sides and bottom.

2 With right sides of the fabric together, sew the two fronts of the raincoat to the back at sleeve and side seams, allowing a 1/4-in. (5-mm) seam allowance. Turn the raincoat right side out.

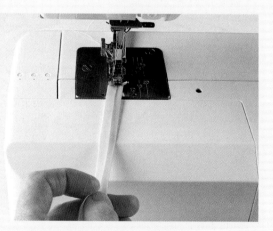

3 To make the belt, cut out a 1 x 10 in. (2.5 x 25 cm) fabric strip. Fold the two long outer edges of the strip of fabric toward the center so that they overlap slightly and press in place firmly using your fingers or nails to mark the crease. Stitch down the center of the belt using a machine zigzag stitch or hand running stitch.

Tip If the belt seems like too much work to make, you could use a 10-in. (25-cm) length of narrow polyester ribbon instead.

Fleecie Pet Accessories

Once your Fleecie Pets are complete, why not adorn them with some specially designed accessories? All the accessories are quick and easy to make, mostly from two-ply yarn or fleece fabric. And since they only need small amounts of yarn or fleece, they are an ideal way to use up the leftovers from your projects, and you can choose to make them in colors that complement your Fleecie Pet's main outfit.

Knitted poncho

You will need
- **Small amount (approximately ¹/₂ oz./10g) of sport weight yarn in your chosen color**
- **Pair of size 5 (3.75 mm) knitting needles**
- **Tapestry needle for tassels**

Note: The poncho is knitted in one piece from the front point to the back point.

Cast on 3 sts. Beg with a k row, k1, inc 1, k1, inc 1, k1 (5 sts).
Next and every alt (wrong side) row until poncho divides for neck shaping, k2, p to last 2 sts, k2.
Next row k2, M1, k1, M1, k2.
Continue in this pattern, making 1 st either side of center st on k rows (right side) until there are 21 sts, ending with a p row.
Next row k10, bind off center st, k to end.
Next and every p (wrong) side row until neck shaping on this side is complete k2, p8.
Turn and continue working on left-hand side of poncho only, leaving other sts on needle.

Work in st st with garter border for 12 more rows, ending with a p row.
Break yarn and rejoin to neck edge on the p (wrong) side on the other side of the poncho.
Work 13 rows in st st with garter stitch border to match other side, ending with a p row.
Next row k10, inc 1 into 1st st of first side worked, k to end (21 sts).
Next and every p (wrong) side row until 5 sts remain, k2, p to last 2 sts, k2.
Next row k8, ssk, k1, k2tog, k to end.
Continue in this pattern, decreasing 1 st either side of center st on the k (right) side until 5 sts remain, ending with a p row.
Next row ssk, k1, k2tog.
Bind off remaining 3 sts and secure loose ends.
You can leave the poncho plain or add tassels. The tassels are made in the same way as the pompoms on the scarf (see page 77). Make tassels at the end of every three rows along the outer edge of the poncho.

> **Tip** To work the decreases on the back of the poncho, check out the information given on abbreviations (see page 13) to make sure you understand how to work the slip, slip, knit (ssk) stitch.

Woolly hat

You will need
- Small amount of sport weight yarn in your chosen color
- Length of contrasting sport weight yarn to make your pompom
- Pair of size 5 (3.75 mm) knitting needles
- Tapestry needle

Cast on 32 sts in your main color.
Beg with a k row, work 12 rows in st st, ending with a p row.
Next row k2 tog 16 times (16 sts remain).
Next row p2 tog 8 times (8 sts remain).
Next row k2tog 4 times (4 sts remain).
Cut your yarn, leaving a 6-in. (15-cm) tail. Using a tapestry needle, thread the tail through the remaining 4 sts and pull securely. Use the tail to sew the back seam of the hat (see page 12). Secure ends. The bottom edge of the hat will naturally roll up slightly to form the brim. Make a small pompom—about ³/₄ in. (2 cm) in diameter—by winding a length of yarn 20 times around a ruler or 1¹/₄-in.- (3-cm-) wide piece of cardboard. Slip the yarn off and tie very tightly around the middle with another piece of yarn. To finish, cut the yarn loops, trim into shape, and stitch in place on top of the hat.

> **Tip** If you prefer, you can finish off your woolly hat with a ready-made pompom. Simply tie the pompom around the middle with a piece of sewing thread and stitch in place.

Knitted cape

You will need
- Small amount (approximately ¹/₂ oz./10g) of sport weight yarn in your chosen color
- Pair of size 5 (3.75 mm) knitting needles
- Crochet hook size 6/4 mm
- 2 beads for ends of ties (optional)

Note: The cape is knitted in one piece from the neck point to the lower edge.

Cast on 24 sts, leaving a 12-in. (30-cm) tail of yarn to make one of the cape ties.
K 4 rows.
Next row k5, inc 1 into next 2 sts, k10, inc 1 into next 2 sts, k5.
Next and every p row k2, p to last 2 sts, k2.
Next k row k6, inc 1 into next 2 sts, k12, inc 1 into next 2 sts, k6.
Next k row k7, inc 1 into next 2 sts, k14, inc 1 into next 2 sts, k7.
Next k row k8, inc 1 into next 2 sts, k16, inc 1 into next 2 sts, k8.
Next k row k9, inc 1 into next 2 sts, k18, inc 1 into next 2 sts, k9.
Next k row k10, inc 1 into next 2 sts, k20, inc 1 into next 2 sts, k10.
Next row k2, p to last 2 sts, k2.
K 4 rows.
Bind off loosely. Work a 4-in. (10-cm) chain of crochet stitches with the tail of yarn at the neck edge to make one of the neck ties. Work a matching chain for the other side of the neck and secure in place. (For information on crochet chains, see page 14.) If you would like, finish the neck ties with a bead at each end and knot to keep in place.

Knitted scarf

You will need
- Small amounts of sport weight yarn in two contrasting colors
- Pair of size 5 (3.75 mm) knitting needles
- Tapestry needle

Cast on 5 sts in your first color.
K 2 rows.
Join second color and k 2 rows.
Continue in garter stitch in this pattern of stripes until the scarf measures 11 in. (28 cm), ending with two rows of your first color. Bind off and secure loose ends.

To make the tassels, thread the two ends of a short piece of yarn through your tapestry needle. Bring the needle through a stitch in the cast-on or bind-off edge of the scarf from the back of your work to the front so that the strand of yarn forms a loop on the back of your work. Now bring the thread over the edge of the scarf and through the loop. Pull fairly tightly and trim. Work four more tassels in the same way. Trim the tassels to about $^1/_2$–$^3/_4$ in. (1.5 cm) long.

Woolly leg warmers

You will need
- Small amount of sport weight yarn in your main color
- Length of contrasting sport weight yarn for the stripes
- Pair of size 5 (3.75 mm) knitting needles
- Tapestry needle

Cast on 18 sts in your main color.
Work 4 rows in st st.
Join contrasting color and work 2 rows in st st.
Rejoin main color and work another 6 rows in st st.
Join contrasting color and work 2 rows st st.
Rejoin main color. Work 4 rows in st st. Bind off loosely.
Join back seam of leg warmer (see page 12) and secure loose ends.
Work another identical leg warmer to complete pair.

NOTE FOR KNITTED ITEMS

For information on knitting techniques, including abbreviations and joining together, see pages 12–13.

Fleece jacket

You will need
- Piece of fleece in your chosen color measuring 6 x 13 in. (15 x 34 cm) (if the fleece has an obvious pile, this should run down the shorter length of the fabric
- Matching colored thread

Create a simple jacket by making a fleece sweatshirt such as Joe the Monkey's (see page 46), omitting the star appliqué, and simply cut it down the center. If you wish, you can also add pockets, which you can stitch in the same way as those on Leapy the Frog's raincoat (see page 71).

Fleece scarf

You will need
- Remnant of fleece in your chosen color

Cut out a piece of fleece measuring 11 x $^3/_4$ in. (28 x 2 cm). Make four $^3/_4$-in. (1.5-cm) snips along both shorter ends to form a fringe.

Fleece courier bag

You will need
- 2 pieces of fleece each measuring 2 x 2 in. (5 x 5 cm) and a 6$^1/_4$ x $^3/_8$ in. (16 x 1 cm) strip of fleece for strap
- Matching colored thread
- Decorative button

Place the two pieces of fleece together, fleecy sides (right sides) outward. Sew around the sides and bottom of the bag using small running stitches, about $^1/_4$ in. (4 mm) from the outside edge. To complete the bag, stitch the strap and decorative button in place.

Fleece vest

You will need
- Piece of fleece in your chosen color measuring 5$^1/_4$ x 9 in. (13 x 22 cm) (if the fleece has an obvious pile, this should run down the shorter length of the fabric
- Matching colored thread

Create a simple vest by making a tunic top such as Hoppy the Rabbit's (see page 41), omitting the flower appliqué, and simply cut it down the center. If you wish, you can also add pockets, which you can stitch in the same way as those on Leapy the Frog's raincoat (see page 71).

Fleece mittens

You will need
- Remnant of fleece in your chosen color
- Matching colored thread
- Length of narrow ribbon (approximately 9 in./22 cm) (optional)

Photocopy or trace the mitten template on page 94 and cut out four pieces. Place two pieces together, fleecy sides (right sides) outward. Hand stitch around the mitten using tiny running stitches, about $1/12$ in. (2 mm) from the outside edge, leaving the straight edge open for the Fleecie Pet's hooves or paws. Work another identical mitten to complete the pair. If you would like your mittens on a ribbon to make sure they don't get lost, simply sew one of them to each end of a length of narrow ribbon and thread them through the sleeves of the Fleecie Pet's coat or sweater.

Fleece pixie hat

You will need
- Piece of fleece in your chosen color measuring 6 x 8 in. (15 x 20 cm)
- Matching colored thread
- Small bell

Photocopy or trace the pixie hat template on page 94 and cut it out. Place the hat template on the reverse side of the fleece, making sure that any obvious pile runs down the length of the hat, and cut out one piece. Fold the hat in half lengthwise so the fleecy sides (the right sides) of the fabric are together. Machine or hand stitch the back seam of the hat, allowing a $1/4$-in. (5-mm) seam allowance. Turn the hat right side out and complete the hat by sewing a small bell on the tip.

Tip For most of the small fleece items, such as the courier bag and mittens, you will get a much neater result if you sew them by hand, as they can be difficult to keep in place on a sewing machine.

Tip When cutting out small shapes from fleece, you will find it much easier if you use a pair of small, really sharp scissors, such as those sold for embroidery.

Angel wings

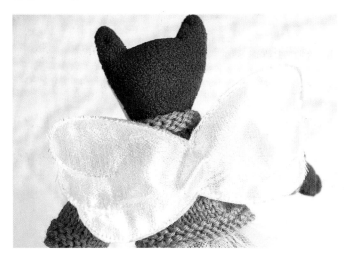

You will need
- 2 pieces of white organza, each measuring 6¹/₄ x 4 in. (16 x 10 cm)
- Matching colored thread
- A piece of thin polyester batting measuring 6¹/₄ x 4 in. (16 x 10 cm)
- Water-soluble pen or quilter's pencil

Photocopy or trace the angel wings template on page 94 and cut it out. Place the template on the right side of one of the organza pieces and draw around it in water-soluble pen, but do not cut out. With the water-soluble pen, add the small lines coming into the center of the wing from the edges of the wing curves, as shown on the template. Sandwich the polyester batting between the two layers of organza. Sew around the wing shape and over the lines, following the marks of your water-soluble pen. Trim the wings very close to the stitched edge and dampen to remove pen marks. Fasten the angel wings to the back of your chosen Fleecie Pet's sweater or top, using a few small stitches.

Necklaces, bracelets and trinkets

You can easily make your Fleecie Pet a choice of necklaces and other items using a variety of beads threaded onto thin elastic or cord. Alternatively, you can make a simple necklace by tying a short length of some of the beaded braids that are now available. Marabou feather trims make beautiful boas while ready-made ribbon roses and other small trimmings available in notions and craft stores can be used on all types of outfits. (Remember that buttons, beads, and other small extras should not be used on any Fleecie Pet that is being given to a child under three years old.)

Tags

You may like to complete your Fleecie Pet with a personalized tag, particularly if you are giving it as a gift. To do this, carefully cut out a 2¹/₂ x 1³/₄ in. (6 x 4.5 cm) rectangle using an index card in the color of your choice. Make a hole at the top with a small hole punch or large needle and thread a piece of thin ribbon or cord through it. Add details on the label such as your Fleecie Pet's name and the date you created it. If you are giving your Fleecie Pet as a gift, you may also like to include a personal message to the lucky recipient. Finally, use a small safety pin to attach the label to your toy.

The Fleecie Pet Workshop

Once you have become familiar with the techniques used to make the toys in the book, you'll be ready to start creating your own unique Fleecie Pets. You can do this, of course, by making your toys in different colors and mixing and matching their outfits. But you can also take the idea further. All the toys featured on these pages have been made using the basic Fleecie Pet body and head shapes, clothes, and accessories and adding a few clever twists and embellishments.

Christmas greetings

For Christmas why not create a troupe of seasonal performers? Santa bear's fur trim is made from a thin piece of white fleece, and the rabbit elf's collar is a circle of red fleece with jagged cutouts around the edge. The belts are made from cord or ribbon. Rudolph's antlers are brown pipe cleaners that have been shaped, poked into the fabric just behind the center head seam, and secured with a tiny drop of fabric glue. His bright red nose is a ready-made ¹/₂-in. (12-mm) pompom.

It's a dog's life

By changing the length of the ears and adding spots, stripes, and muzzles, you can create a range of dogs to suit all tastes.

Family business

You can produce Fleecie Pets in different sizes and even create a whole family of one animal simply by reducing the size of the Fleecie Pet and clothes templates on a photocopier. The rabbit offspring shown here have been made by reducing the templates to 80% and 70% of their original size to create two different-sized children. Some of the clothes are a bit hard to make if they are too small, so it's a good idea to stick to the more basic items, such as those shown here.

Go wild

Design your own breed of Fleecie Pet by combining the basic body with a slightly altered head. The friendly looking lion shown here has been made using the bear head template and adding a colorful woollen mane. The panda has also been made using the bear template. Before finishing, the black ears and white face were seamed in place. The eye patches were added after the toy was stuffed. Other animals you may want to create include a racoon, wolf, or wildcat.

Get personal

For a special gift, why not dress your Fleecie Pet in its own mini version of your relative's or friend's best loved outfit or the uniform of his or her favorite sports team?

Spitting image

Pet lovers everywhere deserve their own Fleecie Pet replica of their favorite pet. This cute bunny is the absolute double of my family's rabbit—but a lot less hard work to look after.

Strike a pose

By threading pipe cleaners through your Fleecie Pet's limbs while you are stuffing it, you can create a toy that you can bend into a wide variety of poses.

Exotic creatures

Create your own fantasy beasts by combining bright fleeces with silky sheers and shimmering stretch velvets. The dog's purple stretch jumpsuit and the turquoise rabbit's tutu are both made like Patches the Dog's swimsuit (see page 18). For the tutu, a length of wide pink organza ribbon has been gathered along one edge to make the skirt. A small piece of glittery braid has been added around the waist, and a ready-made ribbon rose completes the outfit. The pink bear's silver halter top is made like the option given for Squealy the Piglet's bikini top (see page 27).

Templates

All templates actual size

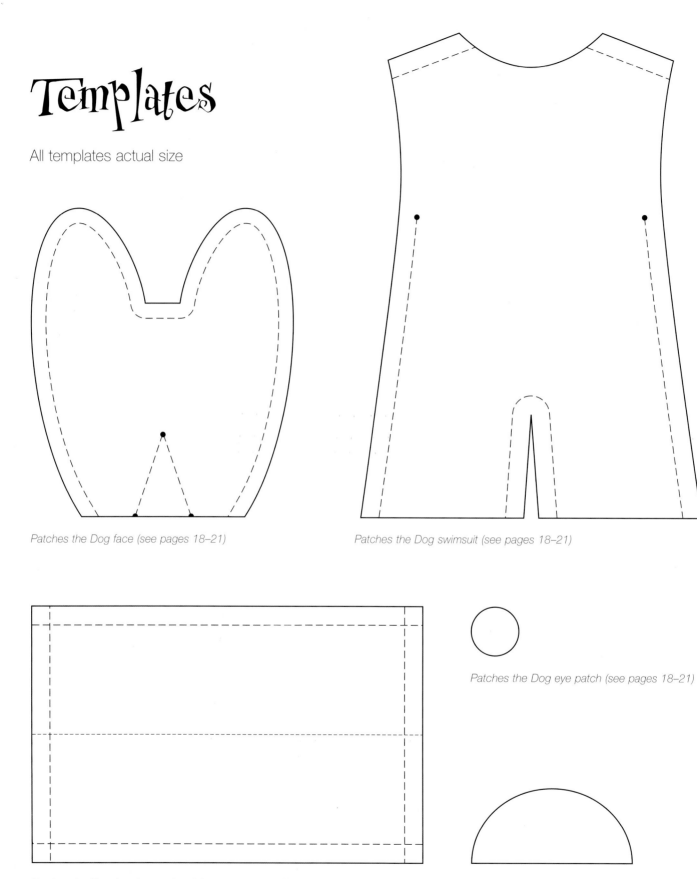

Patches the Dog face (see pages 18–21)

Patches the Dog swimsuit (see pages 18–21)

Patches the Dog flotation armband (see pages 18–21)

Patches the Dog eye patch (see pages 18–21)

Patches the Dog leg patch (see pages 18–21)

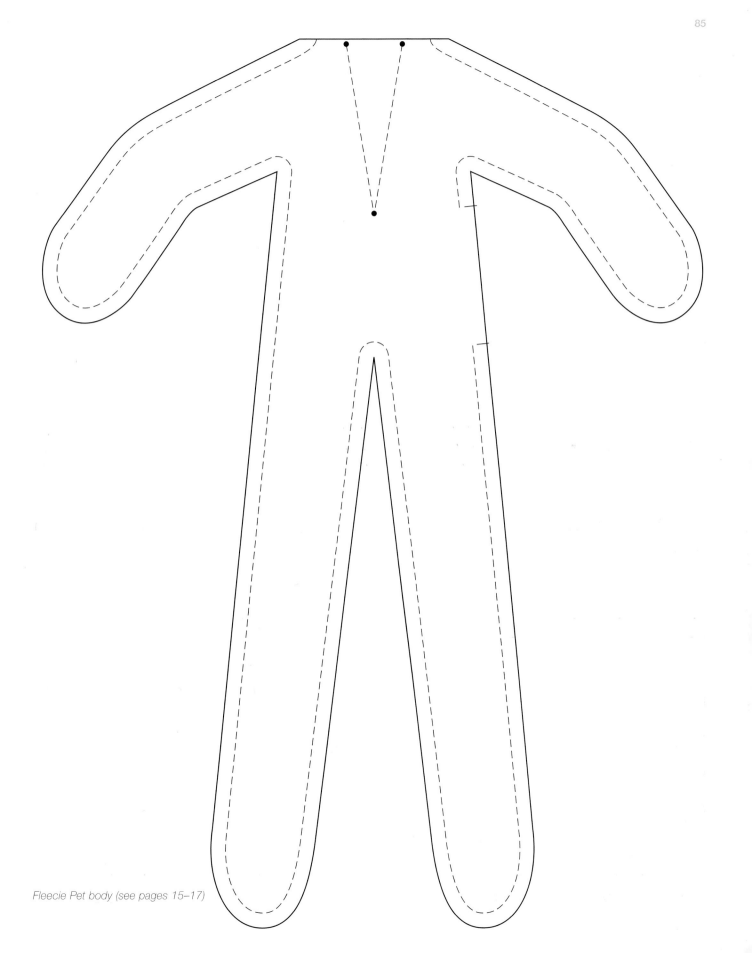

Fleecie Pet body (see pages 15–17)

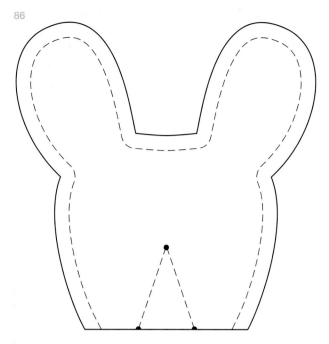

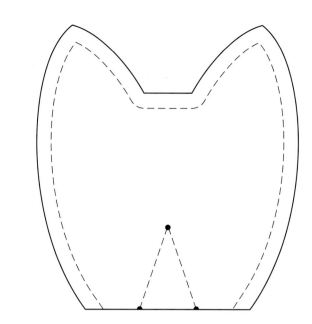

Sniffy the Mouse and Scrounger the Rat face (see pages 22–26 and pages 60–64)

Squealy the Piglet face (see pages 27–31)

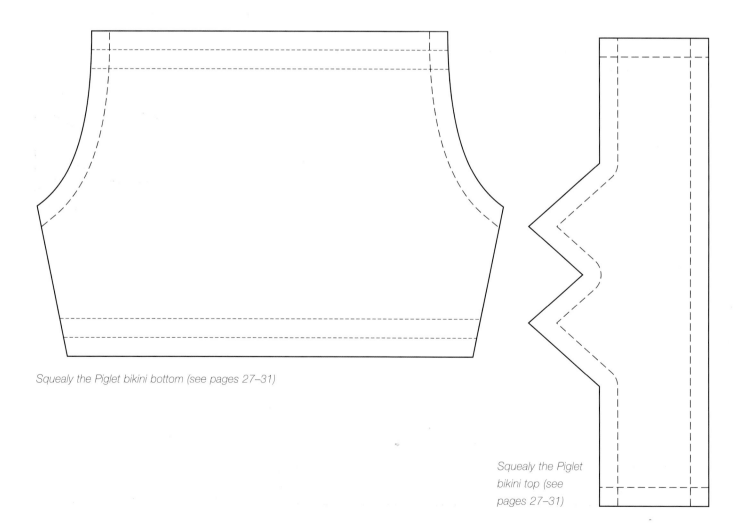

Squealy the Piglet bikini bottom (see pages 27–31)

Squealy the Piglet bikini top (see pages 27–31)

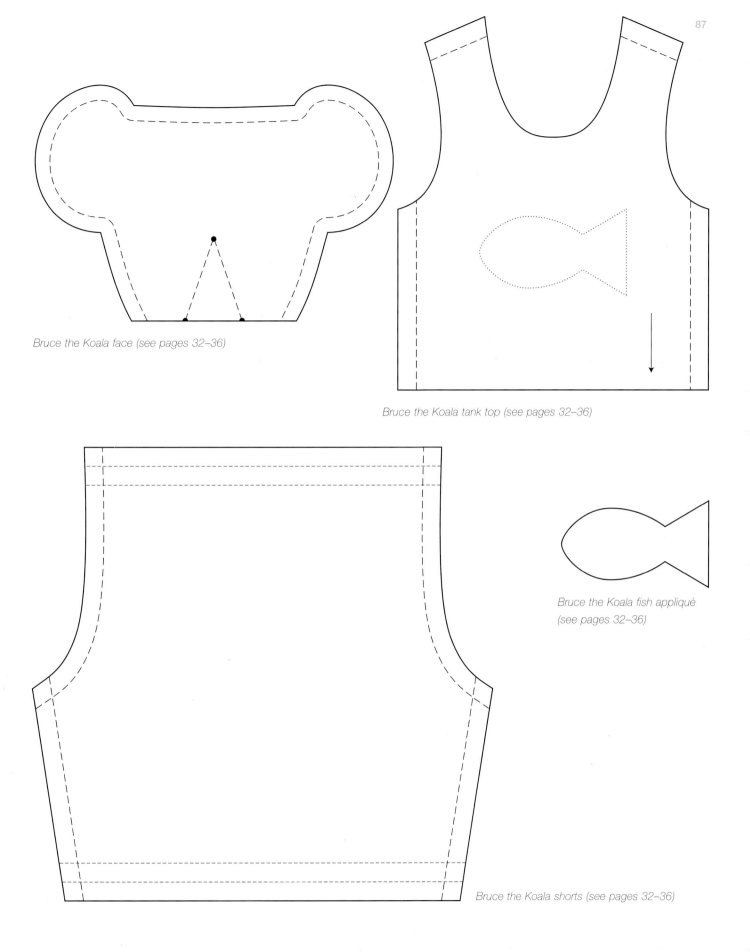

Bruce the Koala face (see pages 32–36)

Bruce the Koala tank top (see pages 32–36)

Bruce the Koala fish appliqué
(see pages 32–36)

Bruce the Koala shorts (see pages 32–36)

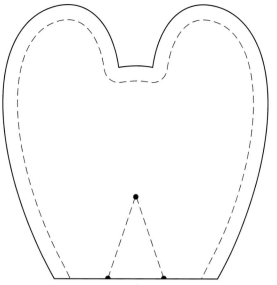

*Snowy the Polar Bear Cub and Rumble the Bear face
(see pages 37–40 and pages 56–59)*

*Snowy the Polar Bear Cub heart appliqué
(see pages 37–40)*

Snowy the Polar Bear Cub dress front/back (see pages 37–40)

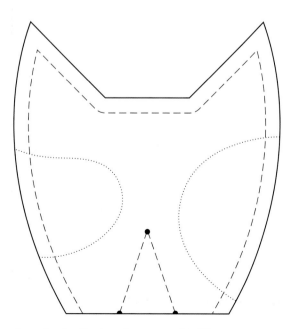

Spangles the Cat face (see pages 51–55)

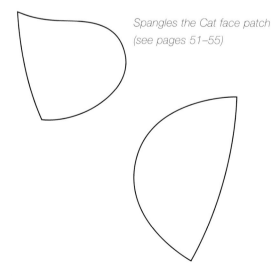

*Spangles the Cat face patch
(see pages 51–55)*

*Spangles the Cat face right patch
(see pages 51–55)*

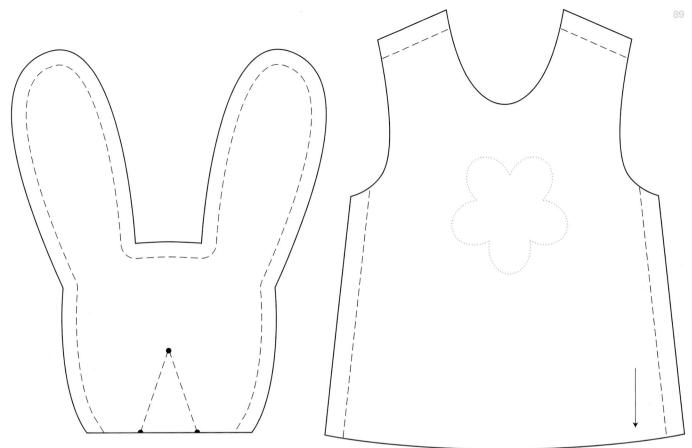

Hoppy the Rabbit face (see pages 41–45)

Hoppy the Rabbit tunic top front/back (see pages 41–45)

Hoppy the Rabbit tunic top flower appliqué (see pages 41–45)

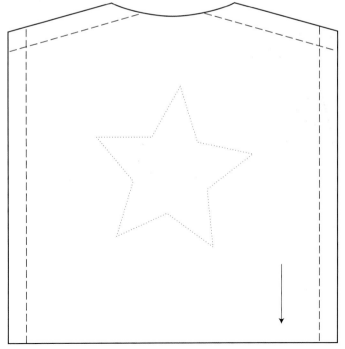

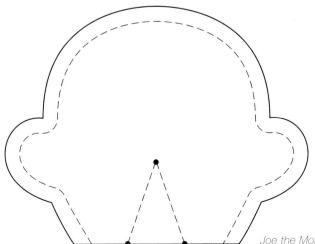

Joe the Monkey sweatshirt front/back (see pages 46–50)

Joe the Monkey head (see pages 46–50)

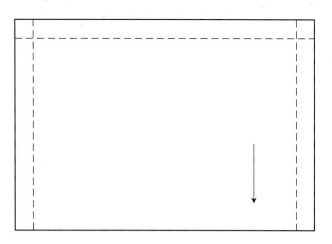

Joe the Monkey sweatshirt sleeve (see pages 46–50)

Joe the Monkey sweatshirt star appliqué (see pages 46–50)

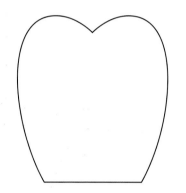

Joe the Monkey face (see pages 46–50)

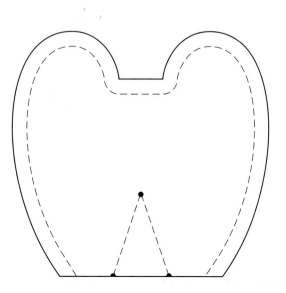

Leapy the Frog face (see pages 71–74)

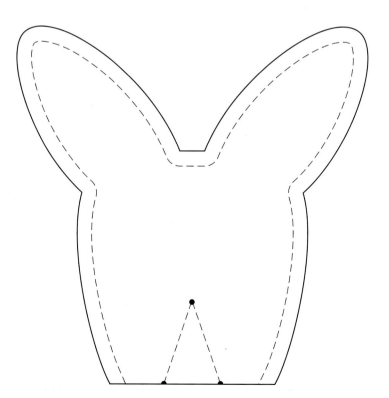

Fuzzy the Sheep face (see pages 65–70)

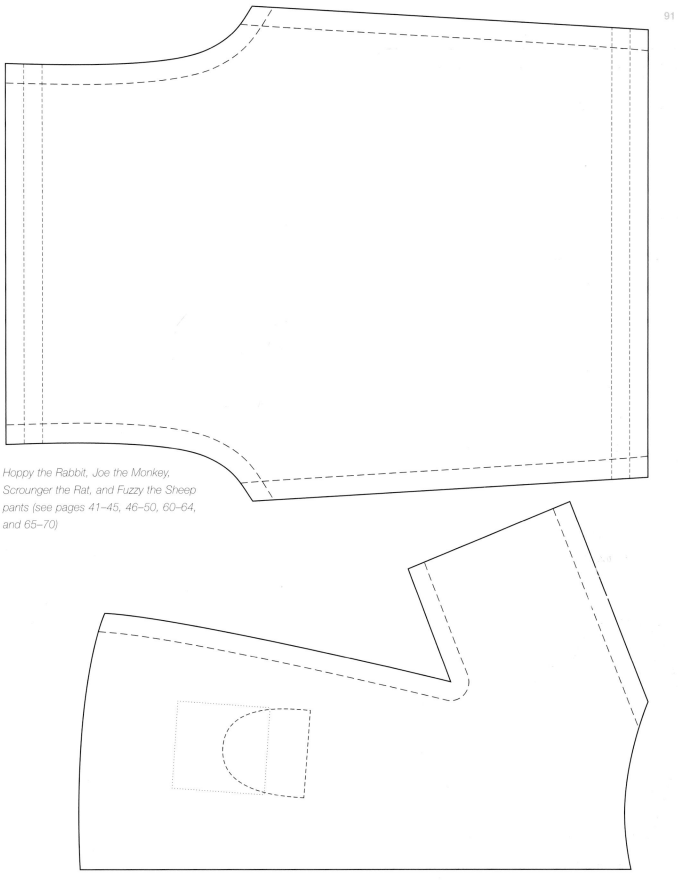

Hoppy the Rabbit, Joe the Monkey, Scrounger the Rat, and Fuzzy the Sheep pants (see pages 41–45, 46–50, 60–64, and 65–70)

Fuzzy the Sheep and Leapy the Frog coat front (see pages 65–70 and 71–74)

Fuzzy the Sheep coat pocket (see pages 65–70)

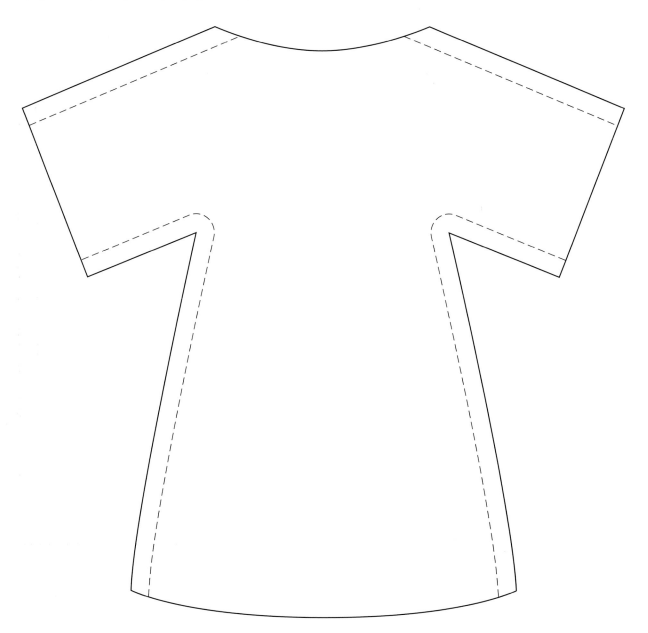

Fuzzy the Sheep and Leapy the Frog coat back (see pages 65–70 and 71–74)

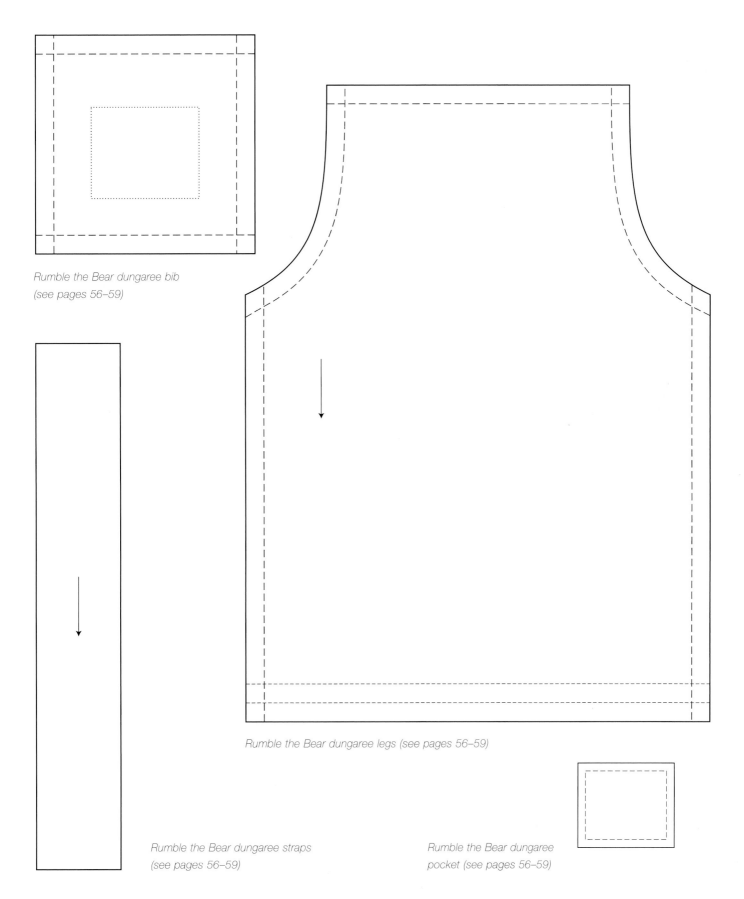

Rumble the Bear dungaree bib
(see pages 56–59)

Rumble the Bear dungaree legs (see pages 56–59)

Rumble the Bear dungaree straps
(see pages 56–59)

Rumble the Bear dungaree
pocket (see pages 56–59)

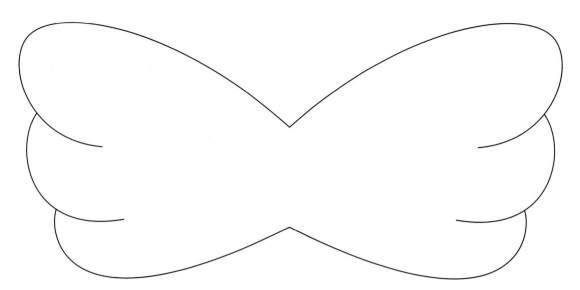

Angel wings (see page 80)

Fleece mittens (see page 79)

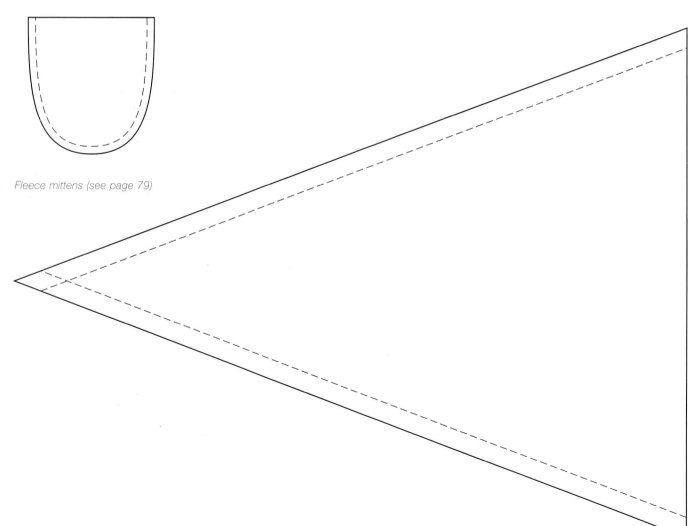

Fleece pixie hat (see page 79)

Index